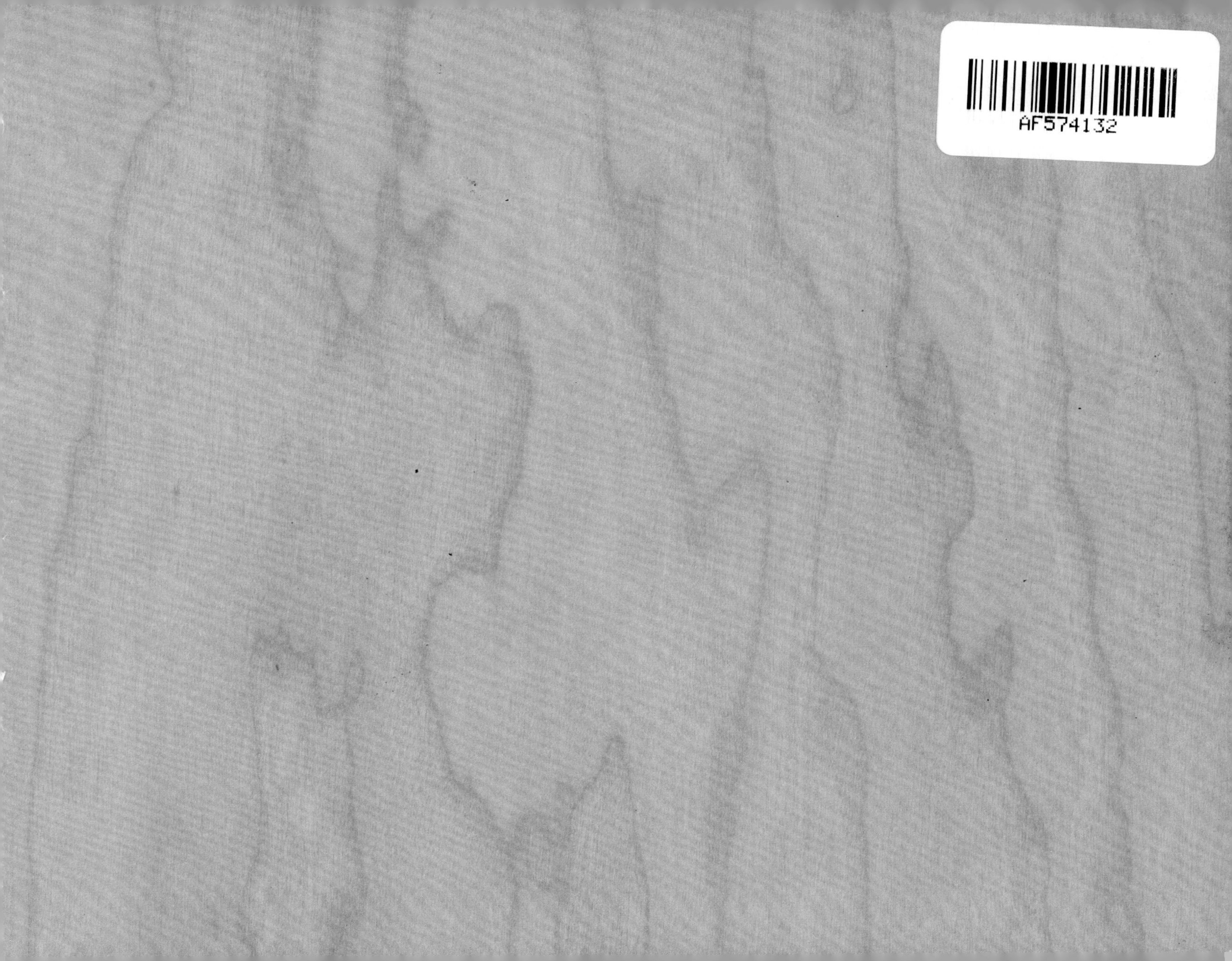
AF574132

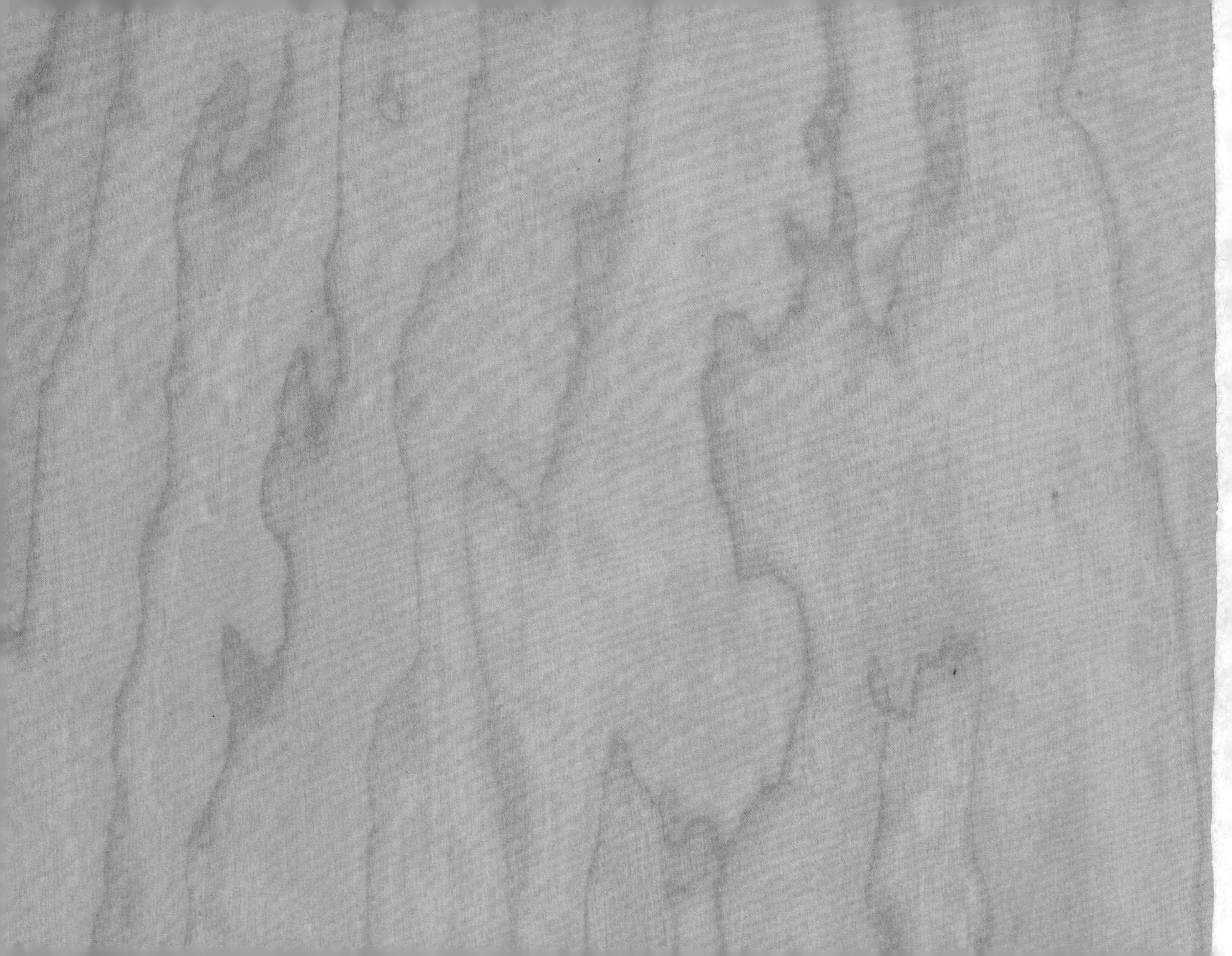

To Sean + Sophia
with much love,
Randi

No Circus

Randi Malkin Steinberger

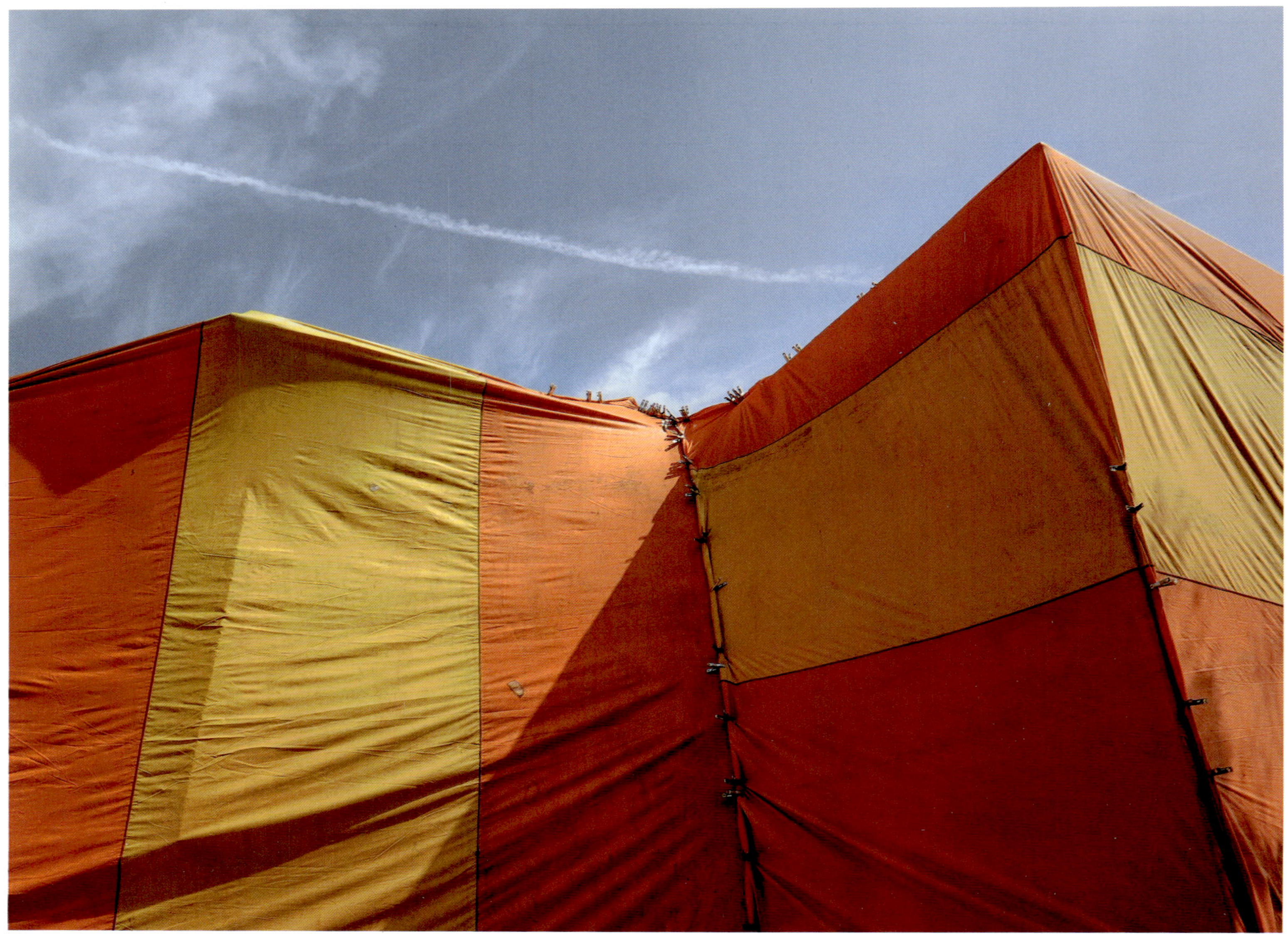

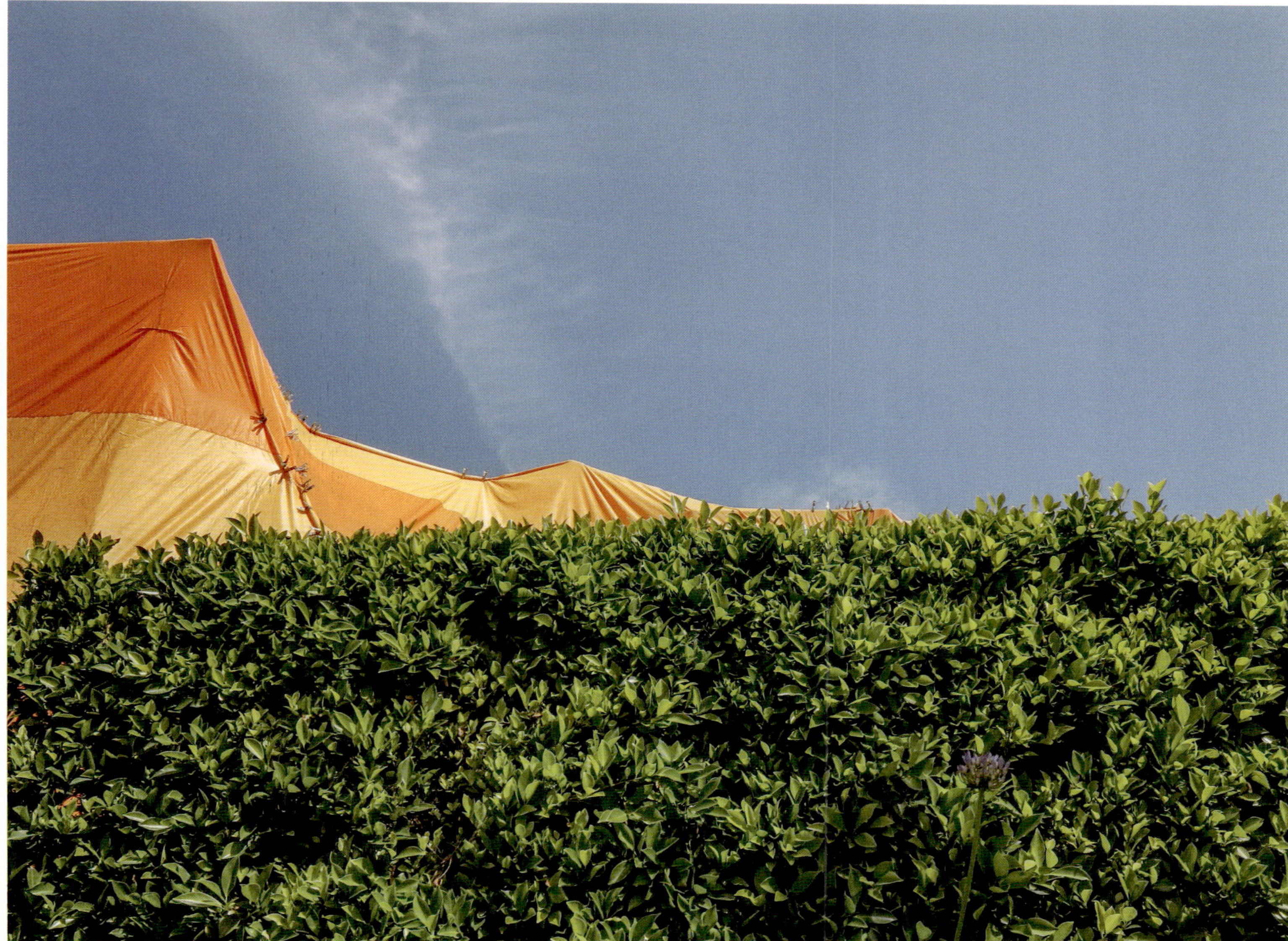

No Circus

Randi Malkin Steinberger

Essay by D.J. Waldie

DJ Waldie
oct 1, 2016

DAMIANI

Shrouded Houses
By D.J. Waldie

The house we are born into is our first universe, "a real cosmos in every sense of the word" the phenomenologist Gaston Bachelard believed. That house may be all that we ever know of poetry, politics, or the temporality of space; the only place where we might have knowledge of what lies behind every door.

If it's infested, the house is quarantined and made into a gas chamber. If it's gone on the market to be sold, the home that faithfully sheltered must be certified by a licensed exterminator as fit to be lived in.

A tented house is the cosmos we're turned out of, a lethal Eden, and the worst of our dreams. Formerly inhabitants, we're made refugees.

A tented house has given up the struggle to be domestic. It's become untenable.

Like some fabulous, fourth-dimensional shape, a tented house has no inside, only an outside.

Its limits have been trespassed, its intimacy profaned, its frailty exposed. It's a carnival spectacle. Strangers now know what's behind every door.

Tented, a house is disenchanted. It's become a premature ruin. It's no longer home. It's a gaudy death trap.

In the early 1960s, as Southern California was assembled into more square miles of places that looked like my suburban neighborhood, only newer, my parents would take my brother and me in their pea-soup-green Ford Falcon station wagon to tour the model houses in newer tracts that invariably had the words "lake" and "wood" in them: Homewood, Lakeside, Woodbridge, Canyon Lake.

My parents seemed ready to buy a house – "getting a bigger place," they called it – but they never did. Perhaps their one move from Manhattan in the 1940s had been enough. Their lives together seemed to be about that too, about the idea of enough.

As a boy, I lay awake nights in the house they bought in 1946 and never left. I was a fitful sleeper, looking up at the ceiling, imagining other

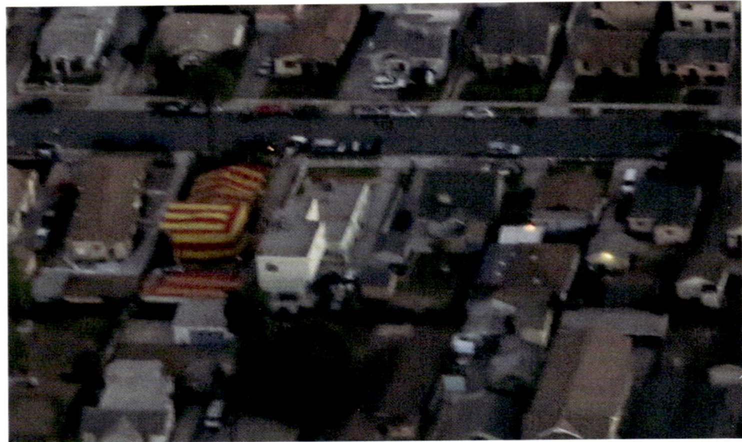

houses to live in. I still daydream of the past's houses-of-the-future. I go back to one of them again and again, past a wall of tan blocks to a room furnished in Breuer and van der Rohe chairs and tables, nothing like the French provincial furniture my uncle gave my parents.

The rooms in real houses betray unresolved ambiguities about how to be at home. How much living goes on in a middle-class living room today? How much dining in the dining room? Perhaps these spaces no longer function as necessary elements in the narrative of our lives, although they linger in our reveries of home.

Closet space is a priority now. The more untethered our experience of home has become, the more ballast we desire.

If you live in Chicago or Cleveland, you may never have seen a house tented for termite fumigation. Drywood termite infestation – the usual reason for tent fumigation in the southern and western parts of the United States – may become more common as the global climate warms.

Termites don't take cold well. Neither do cockroaches. In an evolutionary sense, termites are the cousins of cockroaches that picked up other habits, including a knack for colony formation.

Like ants, a termite colony has a queen, but unlike ants, the colony also

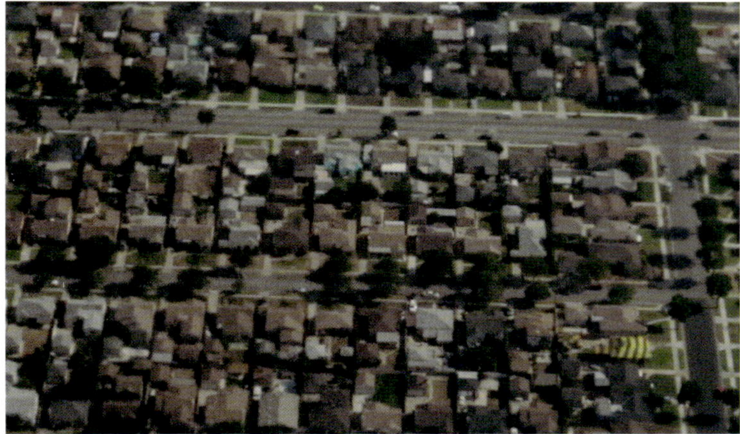

has a king. Once mated, the termite queen and king are monogamous and life-long partners. The queen may live as long as 50 years in some termite species. There is a court of princesses around the queen waiting, infertile, until the queen dies.

Left undiscovered long enough, the termite colony will prosper until the apparently intact timbers of the house are a paper-thin skin over the hollowness inside.

A stake-bed truck arrives with the men. Inevitably when hard, physical labor must be done quickly and with skill in Southern California, the men are Latino. They unload bandoliers of metal clips, bolster-like sand snakes, and the folded tarpaulins.

One of the men climbs a ladder to the roof of the house and judges how best to begin tenting it – a topological problem of covering a three dimensional object with a two dimensional one. The man on the roof unfolds the first of what could be several tarpaulins.

The pieces unfurl down from the eaves to another man on the ground. The man on the roof and the men on the ground begin overlapping the tarp pieces, bunching the edges where they meet to make a seal, and joining the pieces with pairs of clips every foot or so.

The house begins to look as stitched together as Dr. Frankenstein's monster.

On the ground, sand snakes hold down the joined pieces. The ground must be wet so that the weighted edge of the tarpaulin presses into the soil. The completed tent is supposed to be gas tight.

Inside the house, doors that were closed are opened, as are cupboards, closets, drawers, trunks, and chests. If the homeowner has a safe big enough, it must be opened for the fumigator's inspection to be certain no one is hiding inside. The rooms are searched a final time.

Warning notices are posted in English and Spanish on each corner, seam, and doorway.

At the end of two hours, the house is both laid bare and invisible. From the outside, it's a house-shaped enigma. Inside, daylight is filtered into party colors.

A little later, poison, under pressure, begins to fill the empty rooms.

When my mother left our house to die in the hospital nearby, congestive heart failure had swollen her legs and feet, and made her clumsy. She sat on the edge of her bed and could not dress herself on the day she left.

My father was outside, readying the car. I waited in the hallway at the doorway to my room.

I called to her from the doorway. And at the last moment, my mother found a new fear. "Don't come in," she said to me. "I'm not covered."

She called out to my father, who came to the front door of the house. "He can't come in, he would see me," she said to my father, pleading.

My father came back inside to help her dress in a clean nightgown to keep from me the sight of my mother.

Elastec, headquartered in Carmi, Illinois, sells tarpaulins. The tarpaulins are assembled from nylon fabric laminated on both sides with vinyl. The finished tarps could be almost any color, but Elastec offers ten choices: orange, black, yellow, green, white, red, blue, gray, cocoa, and tan. Some finished tarps are a single color, but most are assembled in stripes,

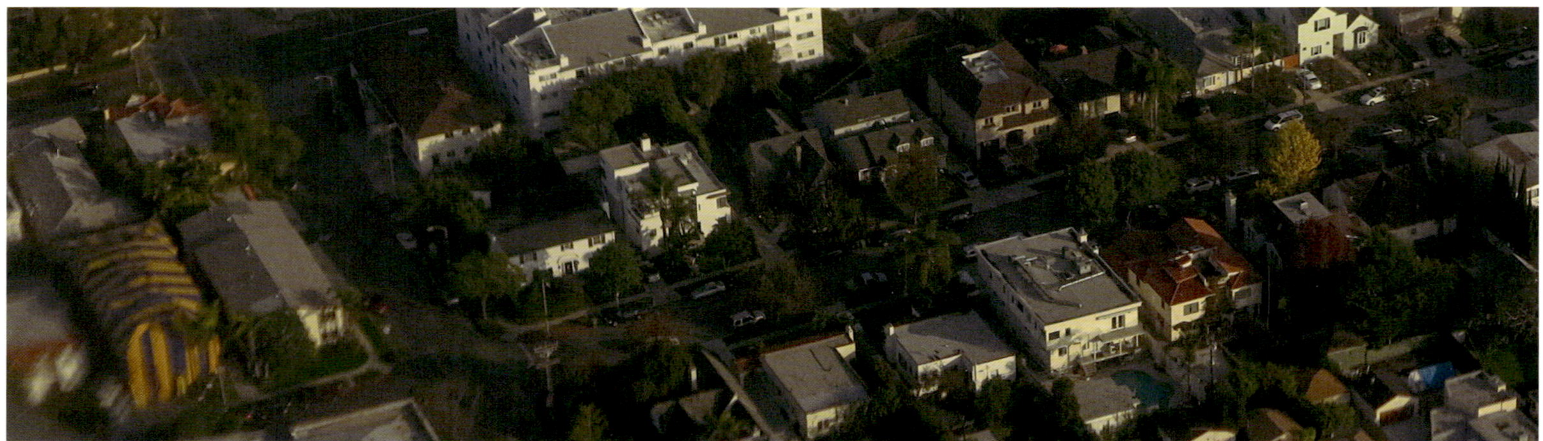

often blue and yellow, red and yellow, or blue, red, and yellow together.

Why tarps are made with stripes of bright colors has two not very convincing explanations. Neither involves circus tents.

The pattern of colors was supposed to be unique to a particular pest control company, serving as a kind of advertisement. Or agricultural fumigators formerly covered rows of fruit trees with wide canvas strips before gassing them, and termiters later sewed or clipped together these strips to make a whole-house tent.

Although colorful, fumigation tents disturb some passersby, perhaps by mistaken association with circuses. There are other associations. Poisonous snakes, insects, and frogs are brightly colored, often in patterns of red and yellow.

Apart from the advertising value of tarp colors, nearly all fumigation companies today hang a business banner on the houses they tent. The Pest Control Operators of California holds a competition each year to award the best design for a banner. The 11th annual contest was won by Killroy Pest Control of Campbell, California.

The judges chose Killroy's banner because it was professional, easy to read and included, Pest Control Technology magazine reported, "a photograph of satisfied customers."

"I think that the tent on a home sometimes scares people, so this banner looks approachable. It makes fumigation look a little friendlier," Killroy vice president and co-owner Richard Schmidt said.

Dow AgroSciences sponsors the banner contest. Dow makes Vikane®, its brand of the toxic gas sulfuryl fluoride, the primary fumigant used to control drywood termites in California. Previously, termiters released methyl bromide gas into tented houses, but it's no longer used because methyl bromide, when ventilated into the surrounding air, accelerates ozone depletion.

Sulfuryl fluoride kills as it breaks down into a sulfate and fluoride in the termite's body. Fluoride is the lethal component, disrupting the termite's metabolism. Its members starving, the colony of termites may take several days to die, even after it's safe for residents to return to a fumigated house.

Other fumigants are more quickly efficient, but they're even more toxic.

Exposure to the levels of sulfuryl fluoride inside a tented house begins with nose and throat irritation and leads to nausea, abdominal pain, and disorientation. These effects may take up to eight hours. Restlessness, muscle twitching, and seizures may follow, if the exposure has been long enough, then pulmonary edema and death.

Because sulfuryl fluoride is colorless, odorless, and initially non-irritating, termiters allow a small amount of chloropicrin to evaporate into the sulfuryl fluoride gas. Chloropicrin, an oily liquid, has a strong, highly irritating odor that causes almost immediate and intense eye watering.

Chloropicrin was first manufactured for use as a poison gas in World War I.

I have an intense recollection of the end of a particular summer day.

I'm very young and I'm playing hide-and-seek inside with my brother. I'm standing in the doorway to the bedroom I would go on sharing with him for another fifteen years. I'm looking for a place to hide.

It's that time in the evening in Southern California when it's still light, but shadows fill completely, as if the light is being condensed out of the air.

The house is small – less than 1,000 square feet – but because I'm small, the room seems large. And I'm afraid. My knees actually begin to knock out of fear.

I'm afraid of what isn't in the room. I fear my own absence.

I went on living in that house with my parents and then, after my mother's death, with my father until his death. After my father's funeral, I returned. My brother brought me back in his car, dropped me off at the curb, and drove away. My house welcomed me inside once more.

That day and over the next, I sat and waited as the late afternoon light drained out of each of the rooms in the house in turn. I have continued to live in that house. I live there alone.

Houses haunt themselves. While we're away, the chair improvises a sitter, the door frame a passing figure, and the bed a sleeper.

A door latch anticipates a hand to turn it, the woman standing undecided before it, her lover daydreaming unaware within, and the life they could have together until they grew old, even the dust undisturbed on the stair tread years after, the light coming through a cracked window of the emptied house, and now a moving van in the driveway.

As the key is set in the door lock by new owners for the first time, as the door knob is turned, as the door sweeps inward, the house constructs a whole life.

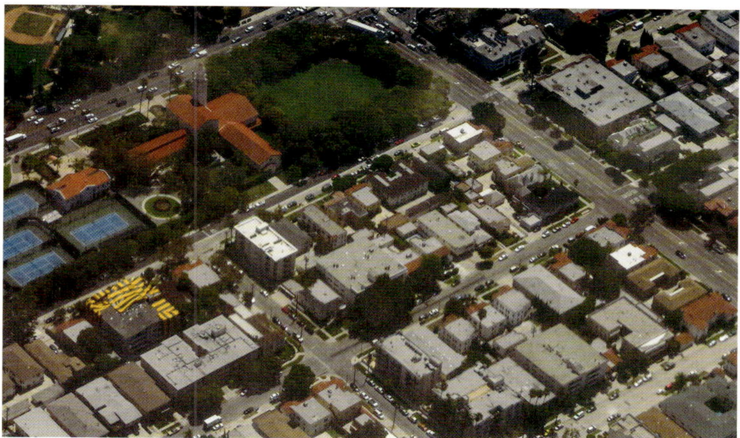

The official who oversees law enforcement in my city warns me that a growing percentage of houses tented for fumigation in Southern California are robbed.

Thieves generally cut through the tent and enter the house by a window, left open to ventilate the gas when the termiting ends. Home security systems also have to be turned off to permit workers to enter and leave unhindered. The fumigation company isn't responsible for security, and homeowners are urged to hire a security service. Some owners park a rented camper in front of the house and spend the next three days on guard.

Burglars take risks too. Some wear breathing masks and goggles to enter a tented house. Other thieves count on the relative safety of the third, least toxic day of tenting. They just cover their mouth and nose with the sweatshirt they're wearing and trust in speed.

There are miscalculations. In 2014, as workers returned to untent a house not far from mine, an intruder was found dead inside. He had apparently died from the gas.

But the appeal of a vulnerable house outweighs the risks. When a man and woman were questioned about a recent burglary by the police department, they said that the crime was so easy, it was "like going to the circus."

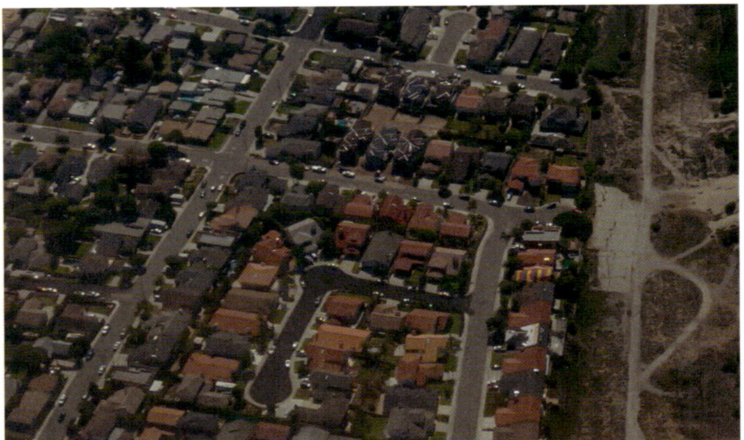

The house itself is sometimes the victim.

Sulfuryl fluoride becomes highly corrosive when exposed to heat. The pilot lights of gas appliances are supposed to be extinguished in a tented house. Cooking and heating gas is turned off at the meter.

In 2002, fumigation workers left a pilot light burning in tented house in Torrance, California. Gas, probably from a leaking meter, accumulated in the tent overnight. The next day, in the early morning, the house detonated. The sound was heard 15 miles away in Santa Monica.

Some neighbors thought the explosion was a terrorist attack. Others thought it was an earthquake.

Some people nearby were cut by flying glass; 20 other houses were damaged in the cul-de-sac where the tented house formerly stood.

Perhaps because I grew up in the 1950s on the edge of one of the nation's largest tract developments, I think about houses.

When I was a boy, I laid out a grid of streets beneath my mother's rose bushes and raised dirt walls roofed with sticks. I had a set of red plastic blocks molded like bricks to build more houses with white windows and doors and a green cardboard roof. I had a model ranch house. To assemble it, I had to bend the sharp metal tabs of wall panels and fit them into corresponding slots. After dinner and homework, I watched *Father Knows Best*, *Leave It to Beaver*, and *The Donna Reed Show* on my family's black-and-white TV: theme music, the opening titles, and sooner or later the exterior of a house a lot nicer than mine.

When I worked for the city I still live in, I used to get calls from Hollywood location scouts. They'd heard of my suburb – the West Coast's bookend to Long Island's Levittown. The location scouts said they were looking for a street of 1950s Americana. What they wanted was the street that Darrin and Samantha or Ozzie and Harriet or Wally and the Beave could have lived on.

I told them that the trees in my suburb's neighborhoods have grown too tall; the houses have gained too many layers after 60 years; and if they want to tell nostalgic or ironic stories of suburbia they'd have to look elsewhere.

London houses are shrouded in fog in books. Abandoned houses (or houses that seem abandoned) are always shrouded by the shadows of overgrown trees.

Houses – in fact, whole neighborhoods – are sometimes shrouded in the webs of thousands of migrating spiders, alarming residents.

The pulverized bits of the World Trade Center towers shrouded lower Manhattan on the morning of September 11, 2001. In secret places, unexamined, that shroud lingers.

Residential towers being renovated are typically shrouded with a woven veil to keep falling debris from reaching pedestrians on the sidewalk below.

Some houses are shrouded for privacy's sake by screens or baffles. Some houses are said to be shrouded by their history.

The ultimate shrouded house – potentially, a house as a shroud – is a fallout shelter.

In 1961, the federal Office of Civil and Defense Mobilization published *The Family Fallout Shelter*, a guide to post-atomic survival costing 10 cents.

In the shelter constructed to the specifications of the OCDM, the father is supposed to give each family member a daily task to perform. A 24-hour watch should be maintained, with sleeping and waking shifts. Everyone should be prepared to stay in the shelter for 14 days. To break the monotony, it may be necessary for the father to invent tasks. Everyone can keep a diary. Someone should monitor the two CONELRAD radio frequencies (conveniently marked at 640 AM and 1240 AM on the dial). Someone should record the reports in a log.

My parents never considered building a fallout shelter, nor did any of our neighbors in our suburban neighborhood.

Fled from, sealed up, pumped full of poison, abandoned by everyone except opportunistic thieves, the tented house waits like Lazarus in his tomb. The nights are darker there. The sun only half lights the rooms.

To be something more than a windbreak or a covering from rain or a frail barrier, a home must have dreamers inside. A house undreamed in is already neglected.

Houses and those who live in them are mutualistic. They share a form of symbiosis in which two different species benefit from their coexistence. Its inhabitants invest shelter in their house. Their house generously gives them habits of living.

Dwelling describes both the shelter and the sheltered. Apart, both the unhoused and the uninhabited are at terrible risk.

Under California regulations, a fumigated house must be tented for a minimum of three days.

On the second day, a fumigator (wearing self-contained breathing apparatus) exposes the house and starts up fans to ventilate the gas. On the third day, the workmen return.

They remove the locks that had prevented anyone but them from entering by the front and rear doors. They carefully measure any lingering toxicity in the air. They turn off the fans that have been ventilating the otherwise silent rooms. They take down the warning signs. They unclip the tarps. They unsheathe the house.

The removal of the tarps declares that the house, after days of being a danger, is safe enough again.

The inhabitants come back to unbag cereal boxes, refill the refrigerator, and let the dog loose in the yard. They close up closets, give rooms the

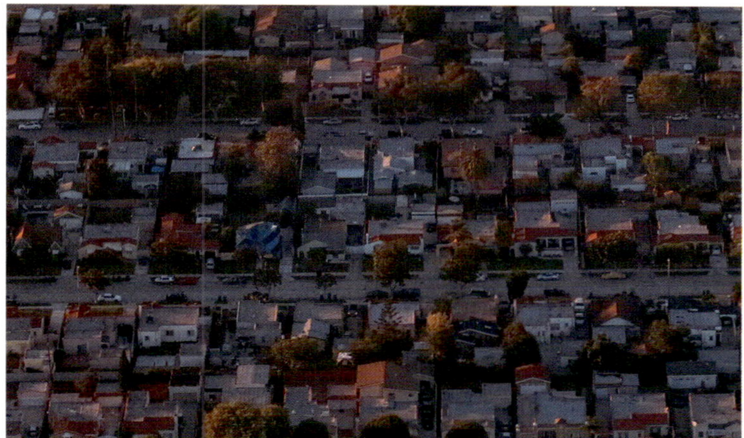

privacy they require, and check to see if anything has gone missing while they were missing. They may pause in the business of rekindling their presence, but not sharing their anxiety with each other, to consider if the deadly gas might continue to pool somewhere inside still. It has happened.

The inhabitants try to act as if nothing but annoyance has interrupted the pattern of their lives together. They try to act as if their house had not been a desolation or a portent of worse departures.

They decline to answer the question their tented house asked. They do not consider how they will live in a world with no shelter.

Ravoli Dr.

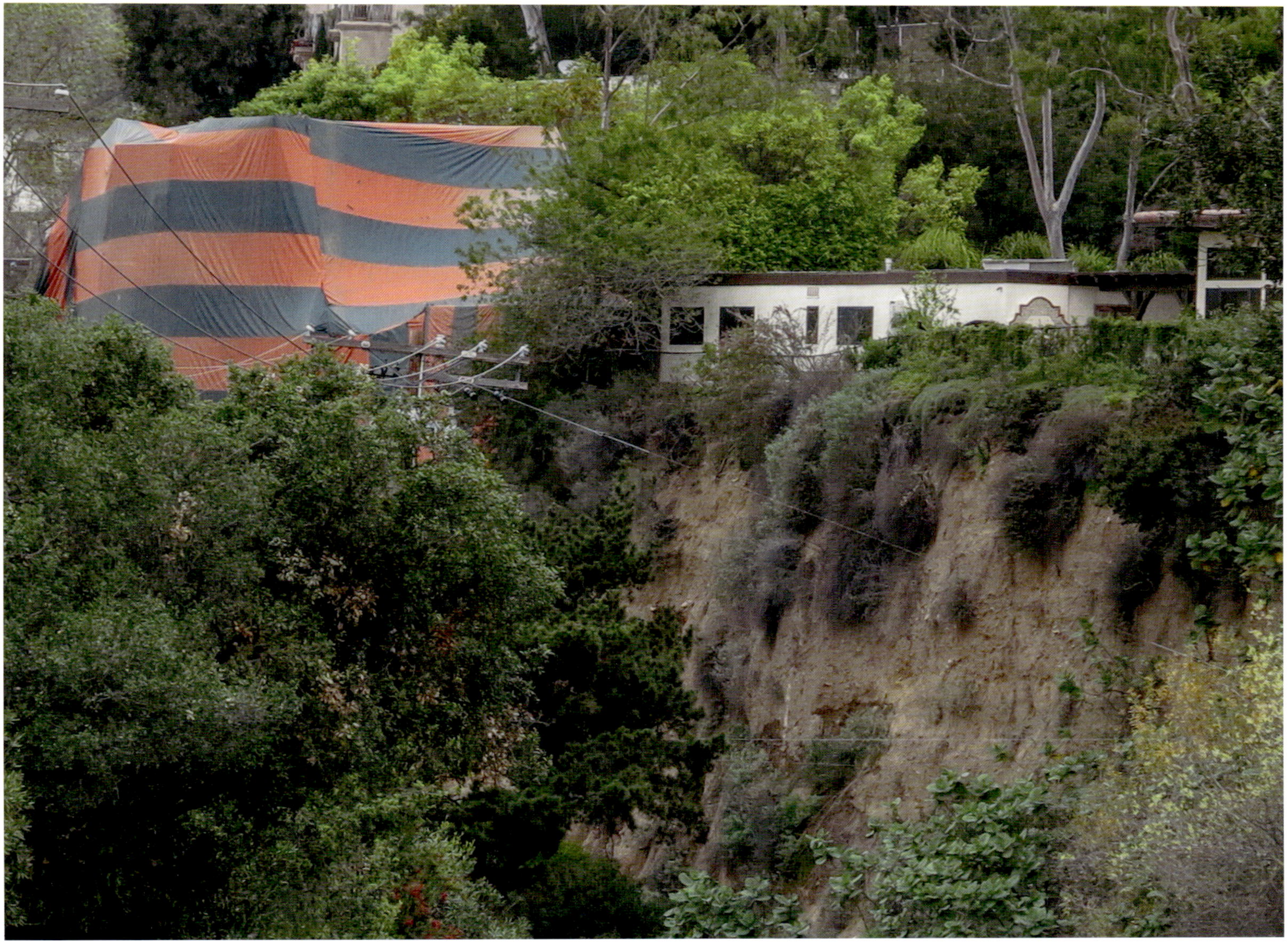

7th St.

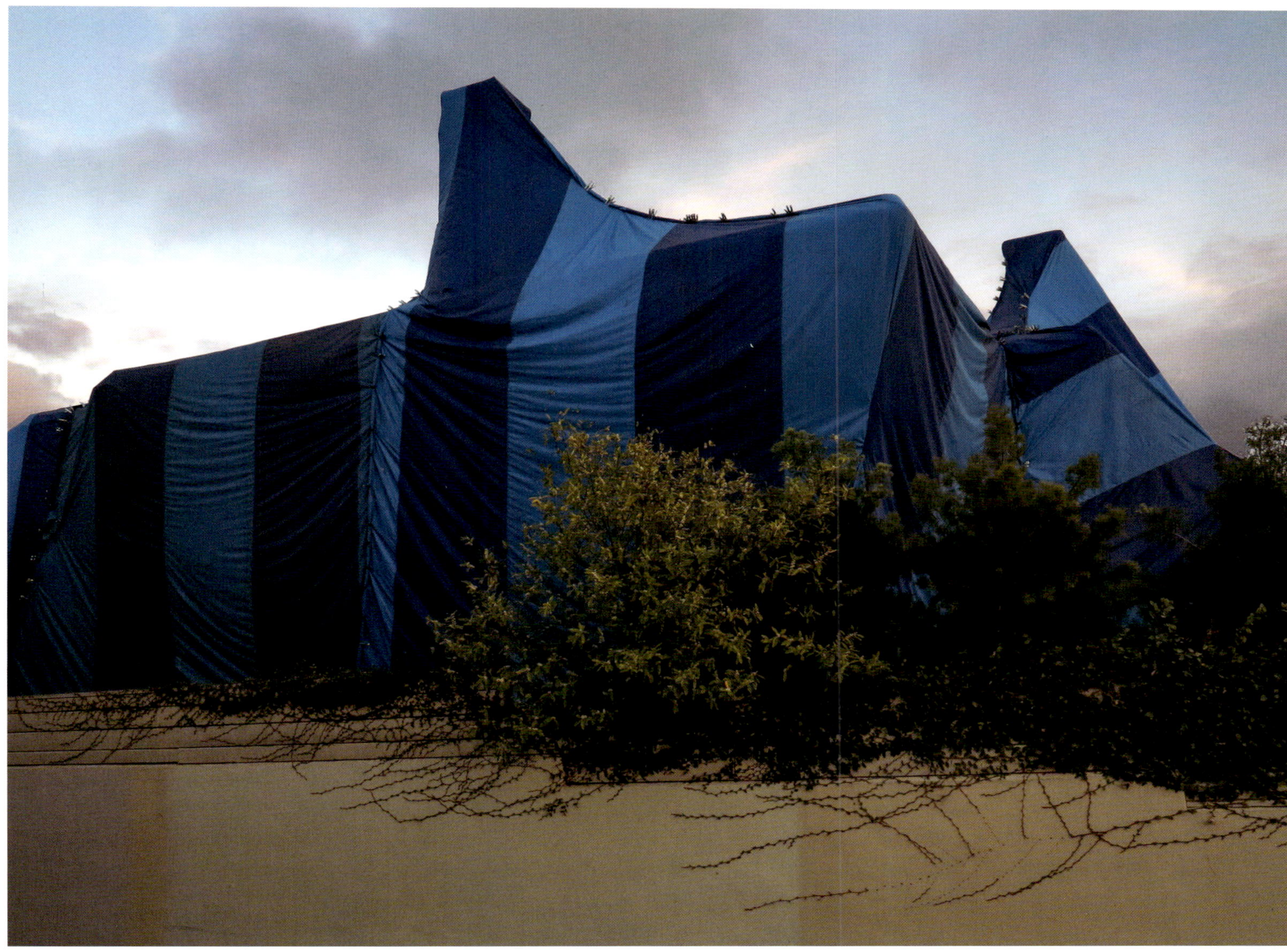

4th St.

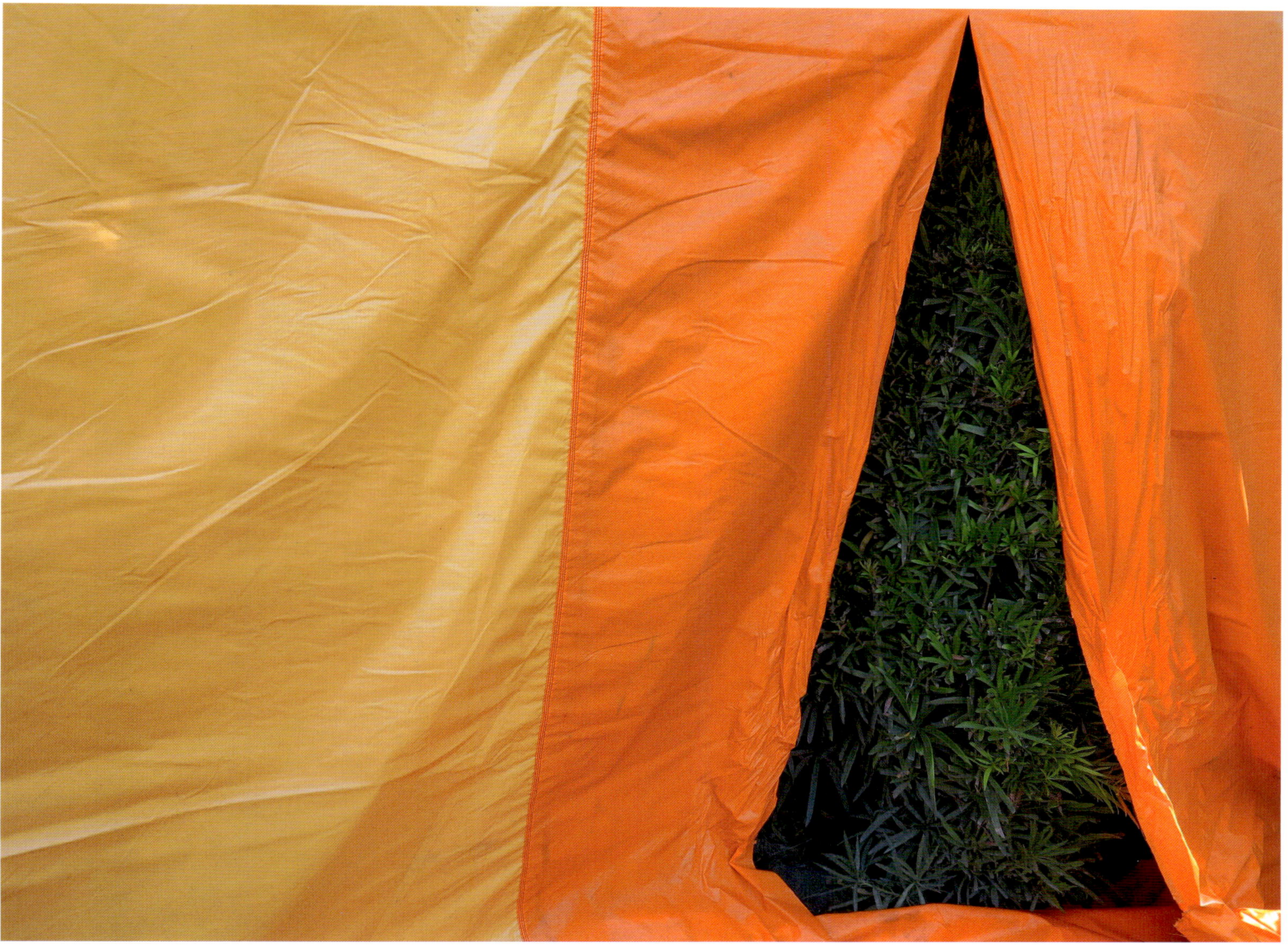

Riviera Ave.

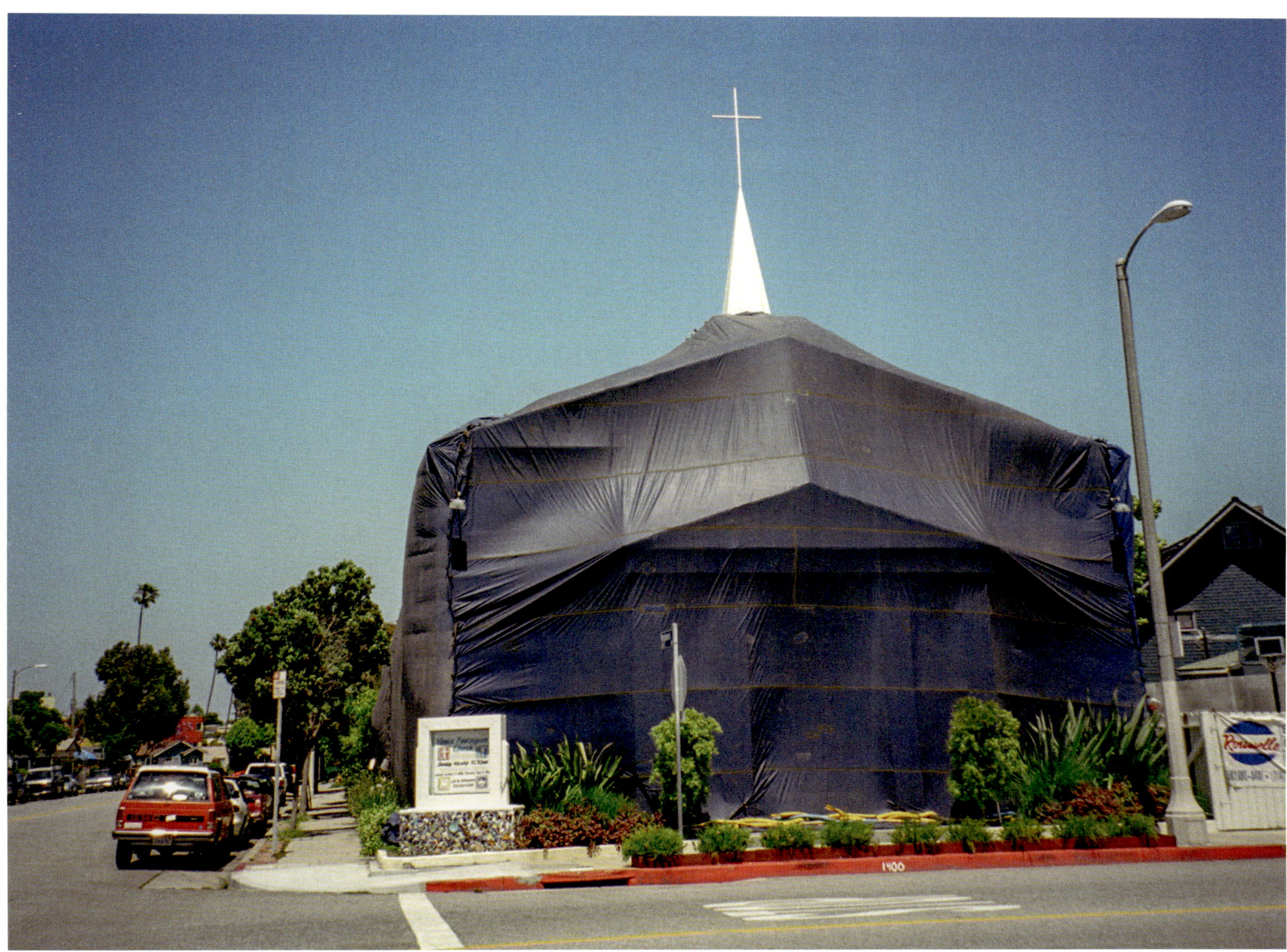
1400

Pier Ave.

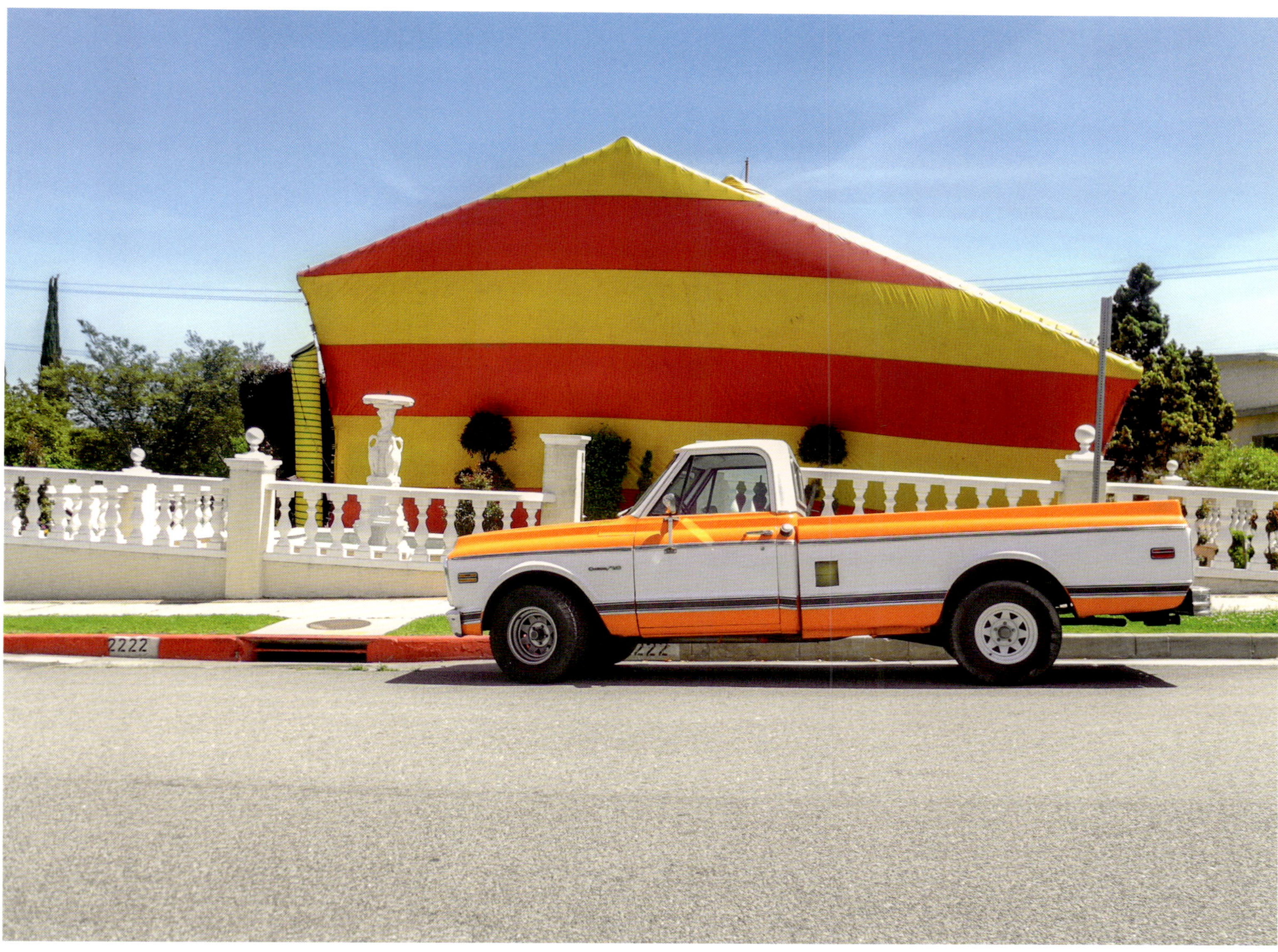
2222

7th St.

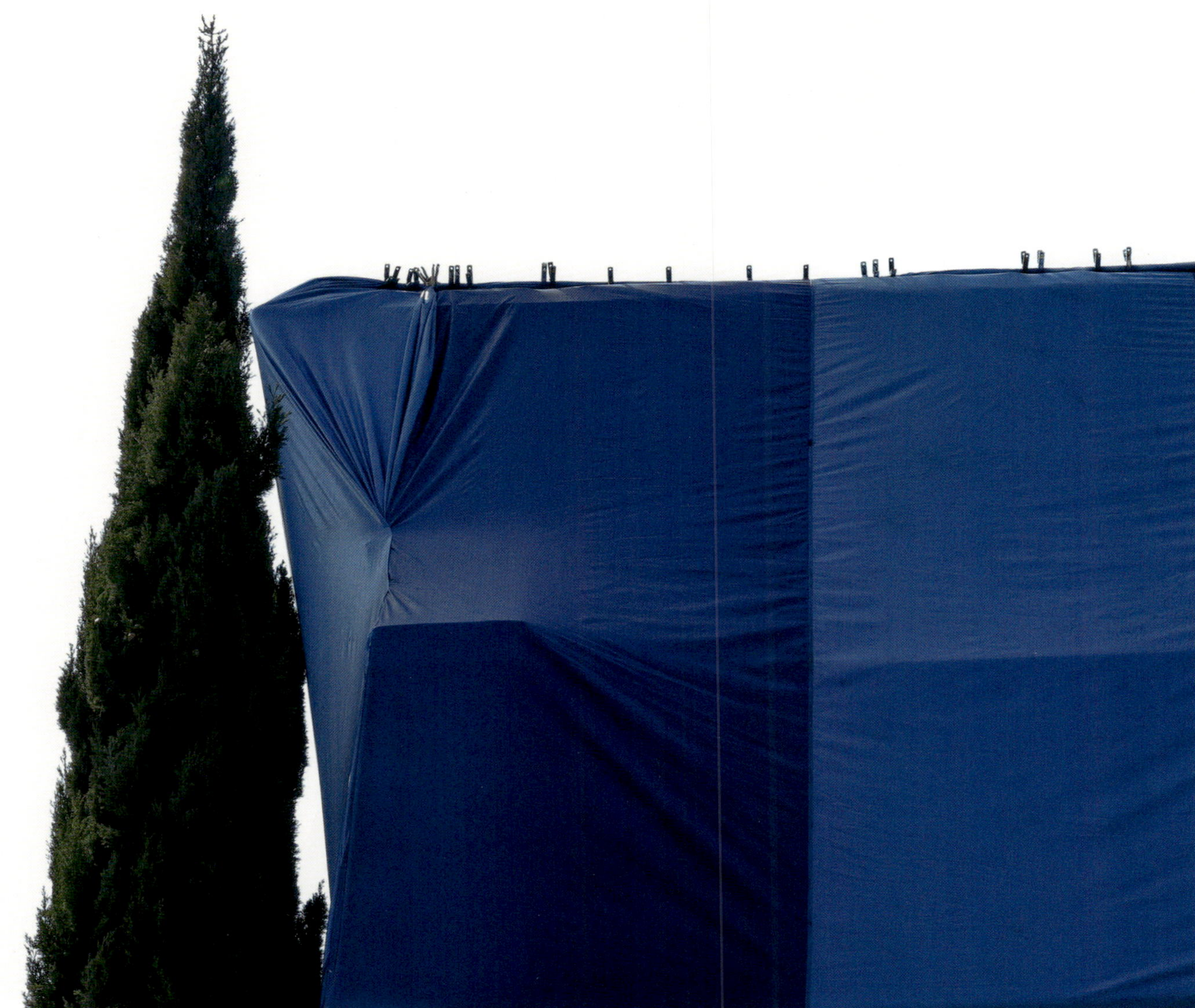

Berkeley St.

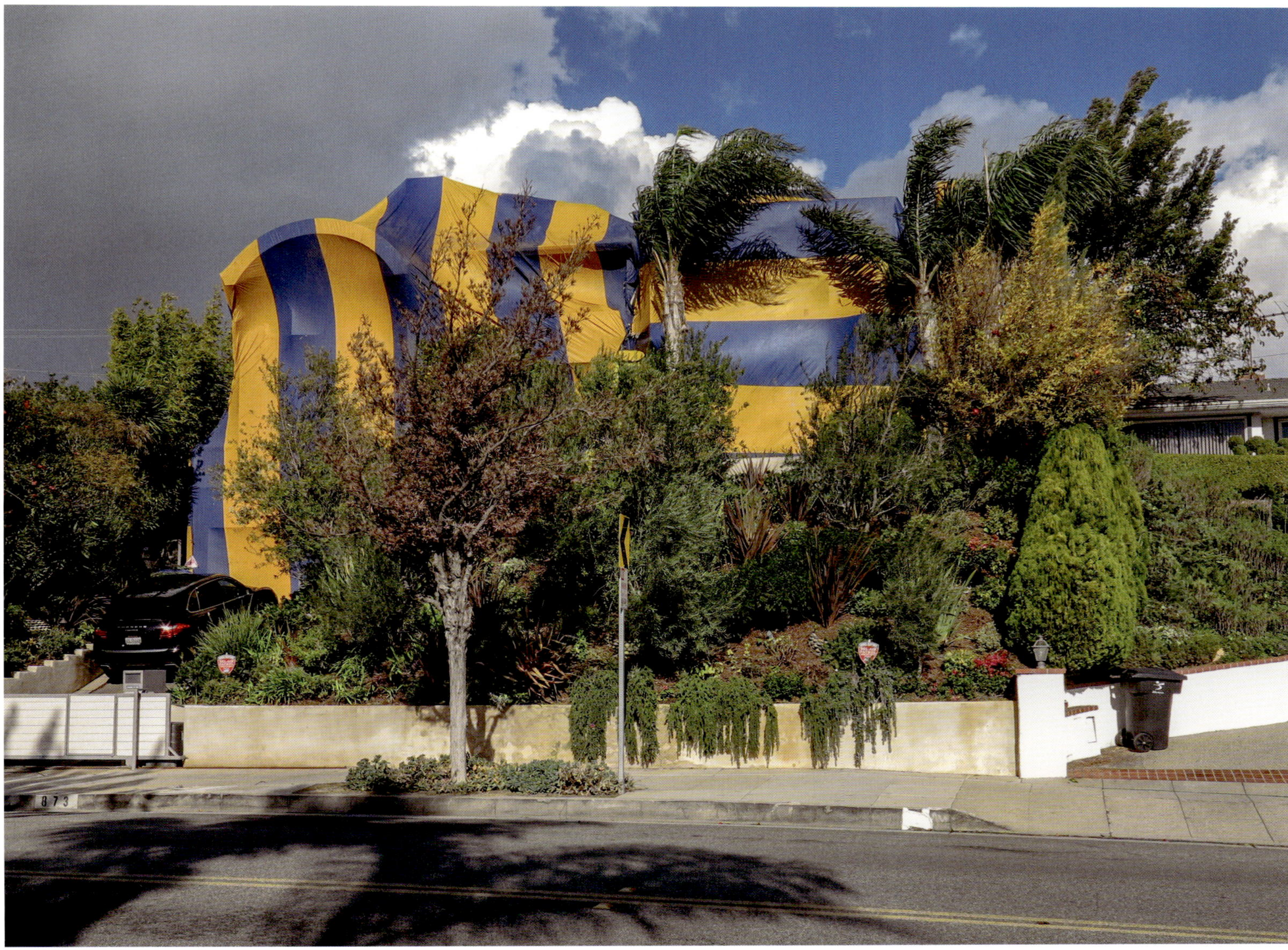

Brinkley Ave.

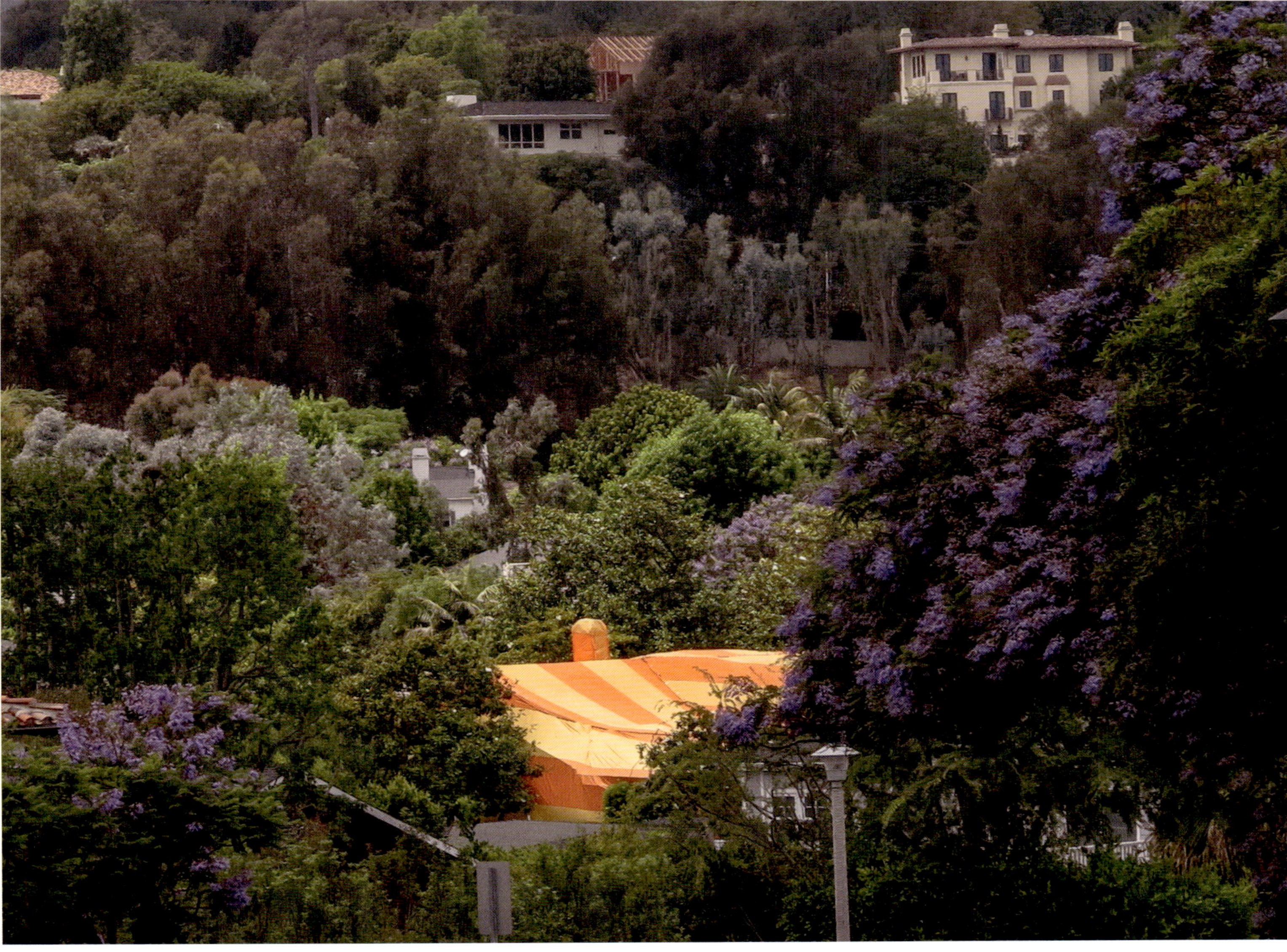

Pickford St.

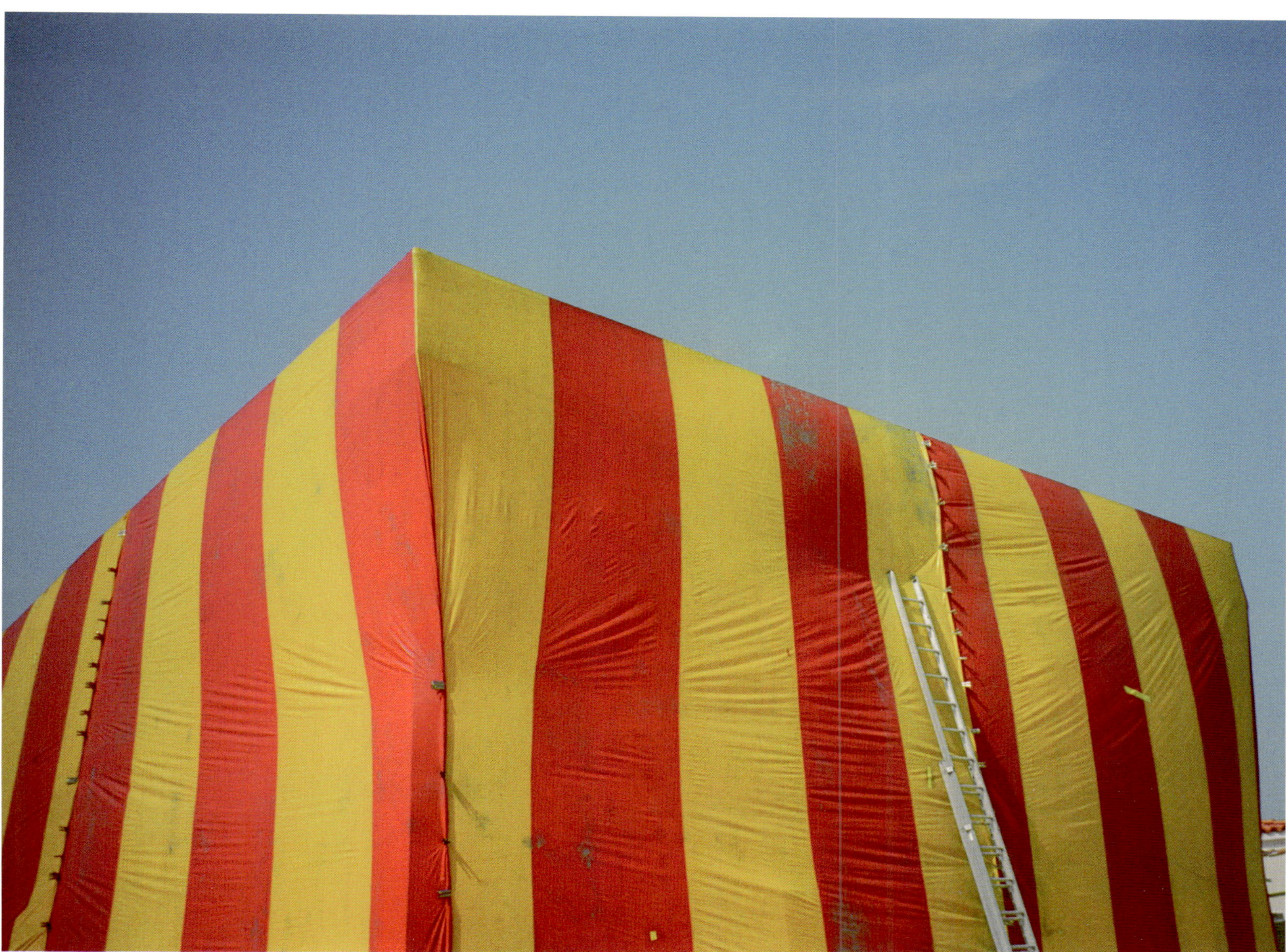

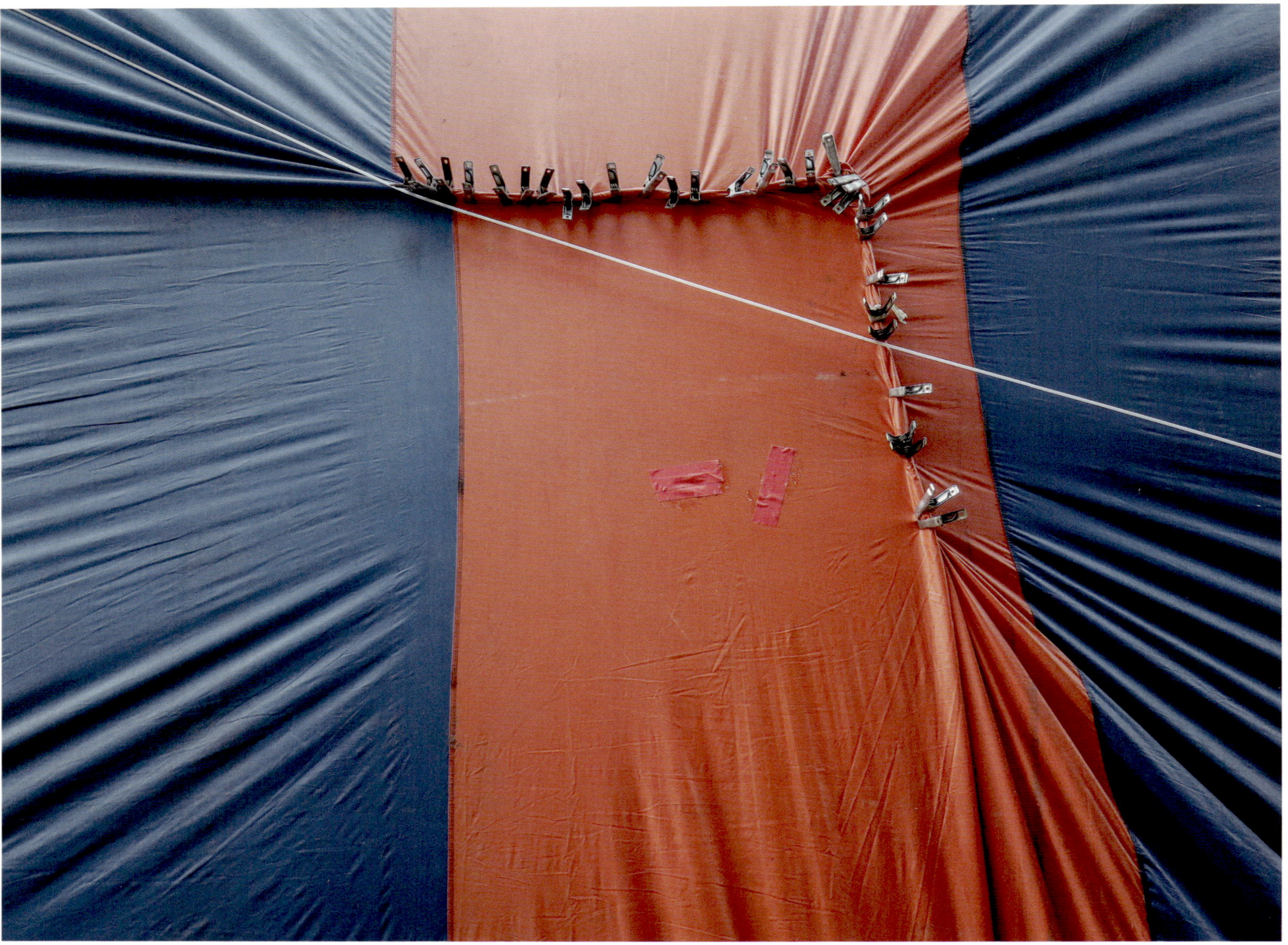

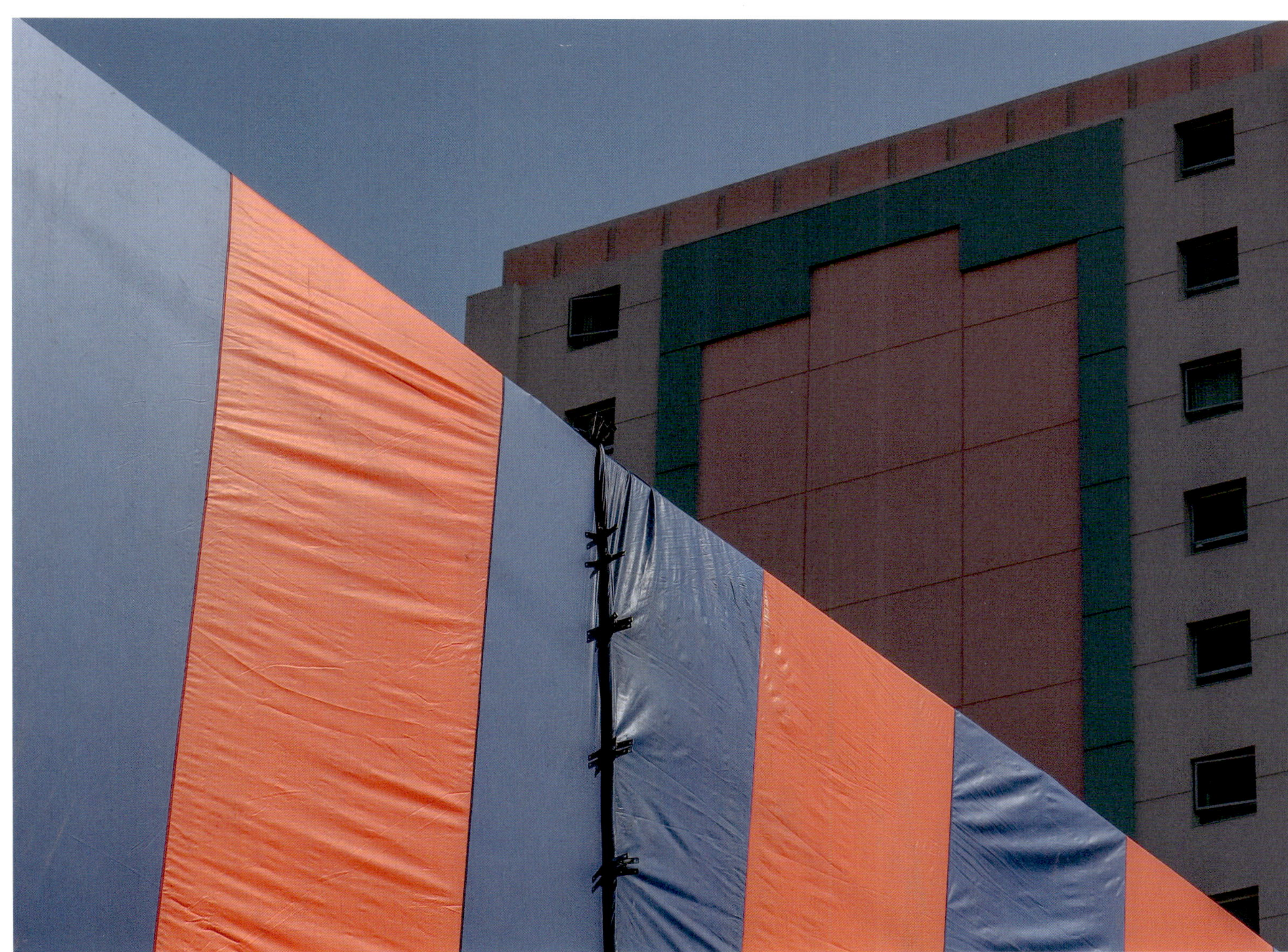

Montana Ave.

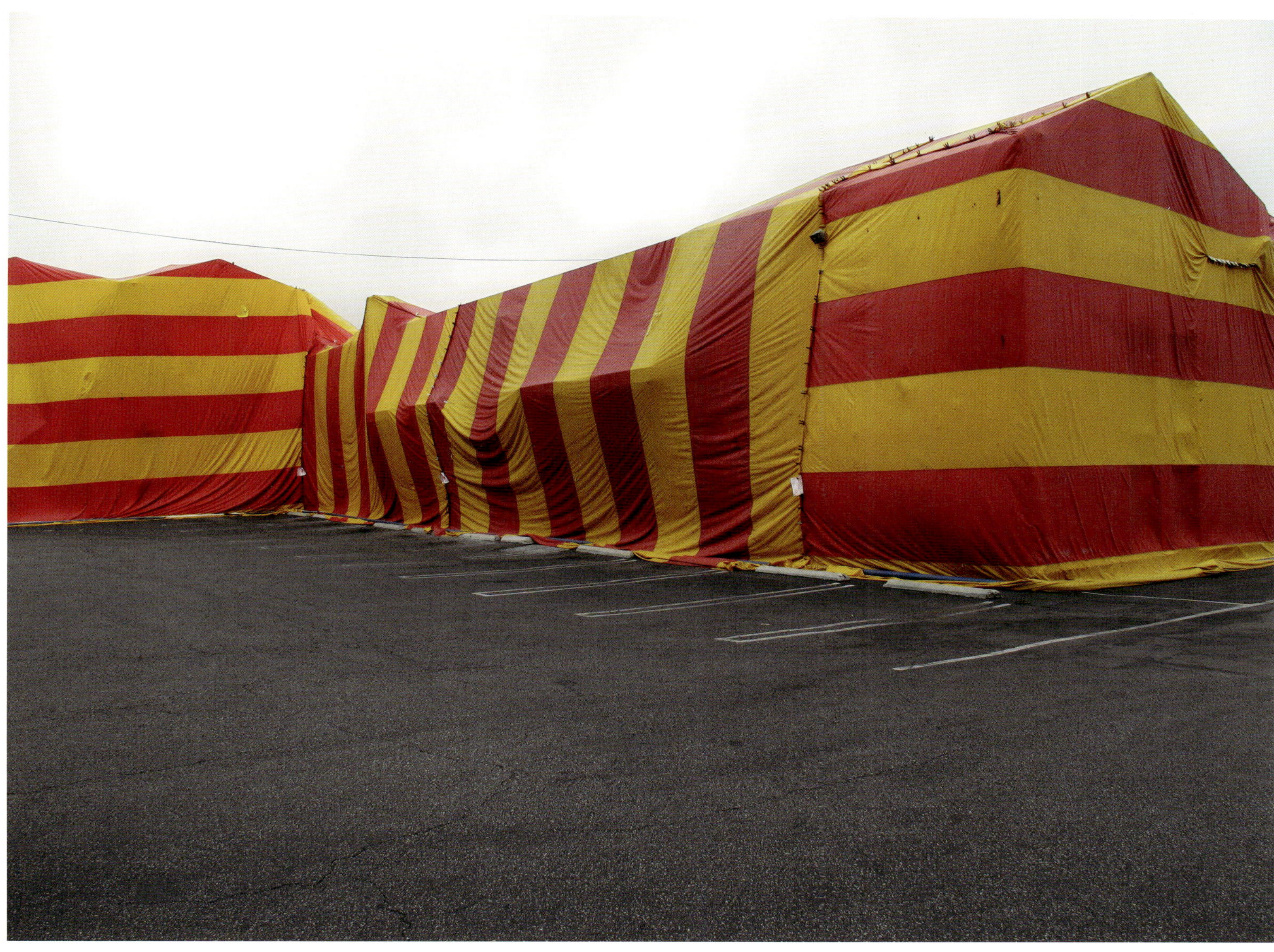

Caswell Ave.

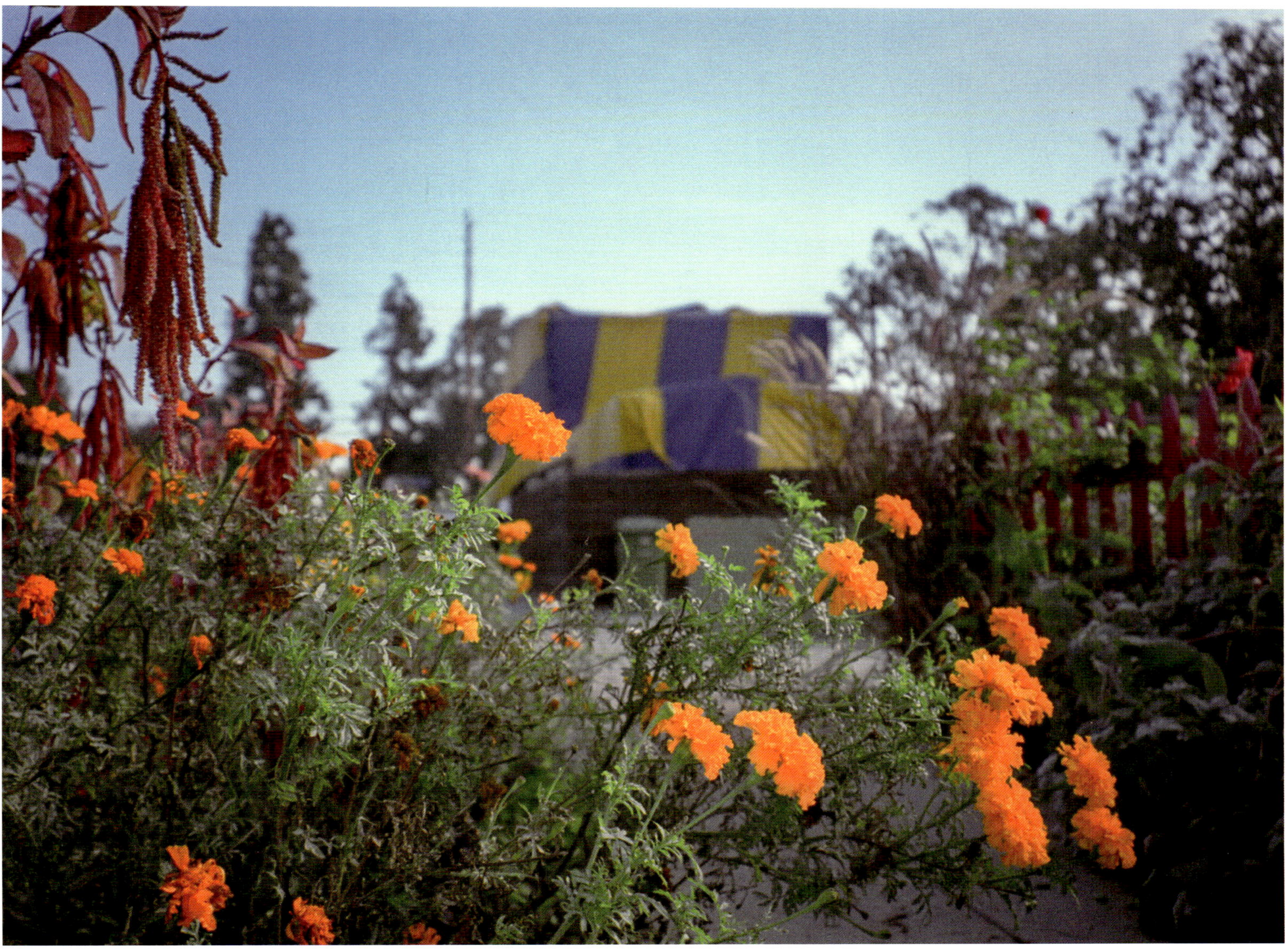

Nowita Pl.

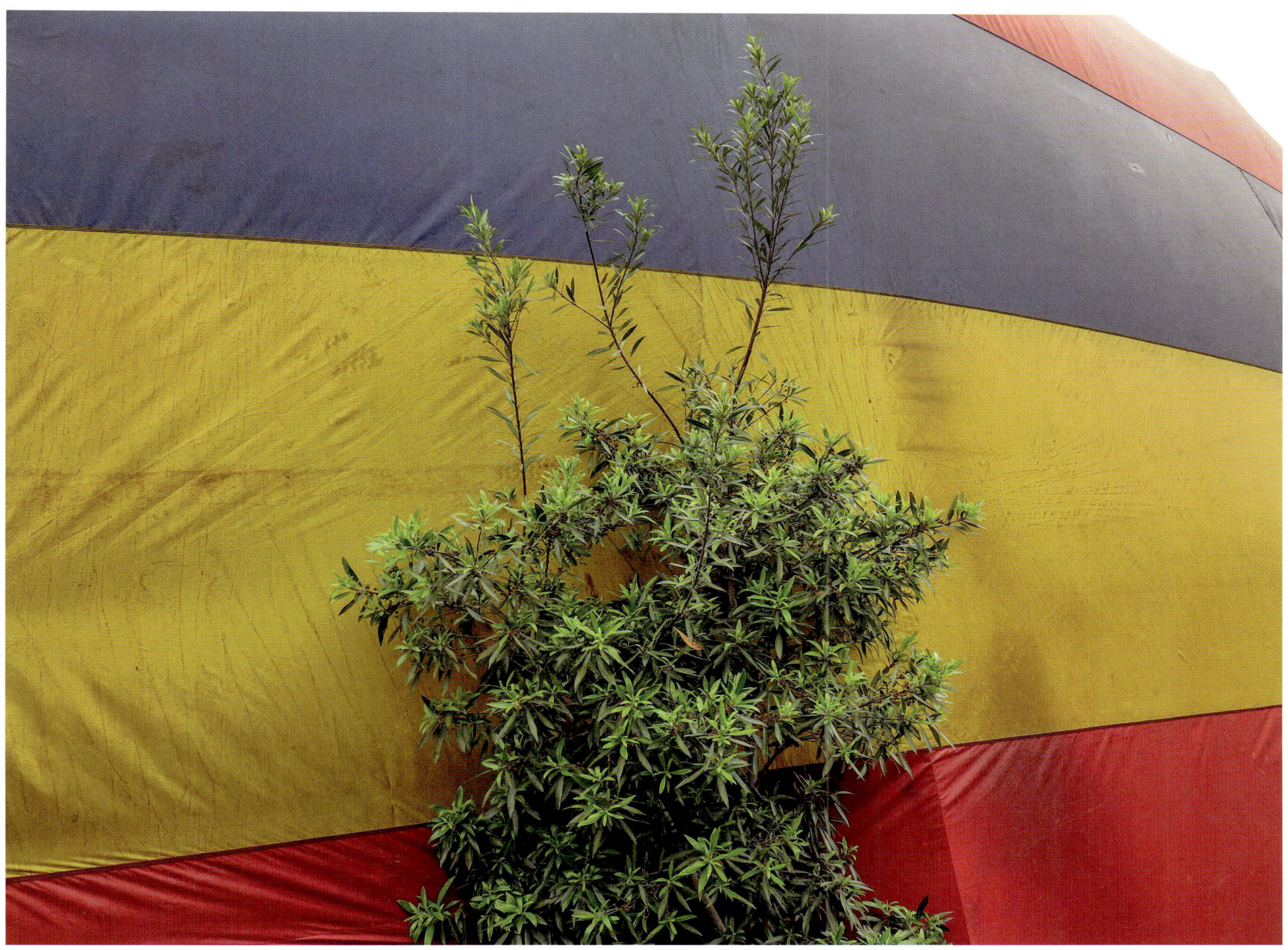

Olympic Blvd.

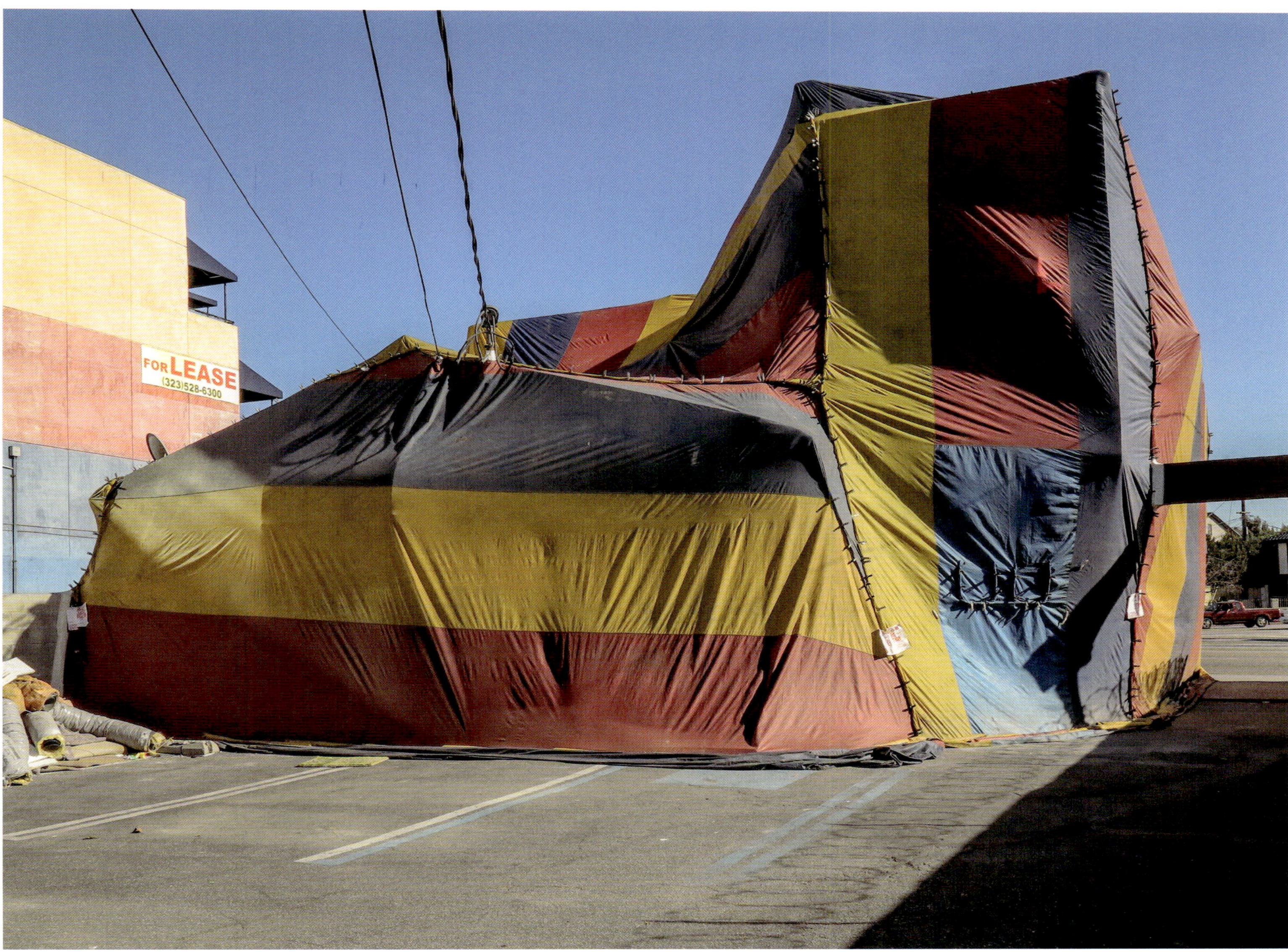
FOR LEASE
(323)528-6300

Lipton Ave.

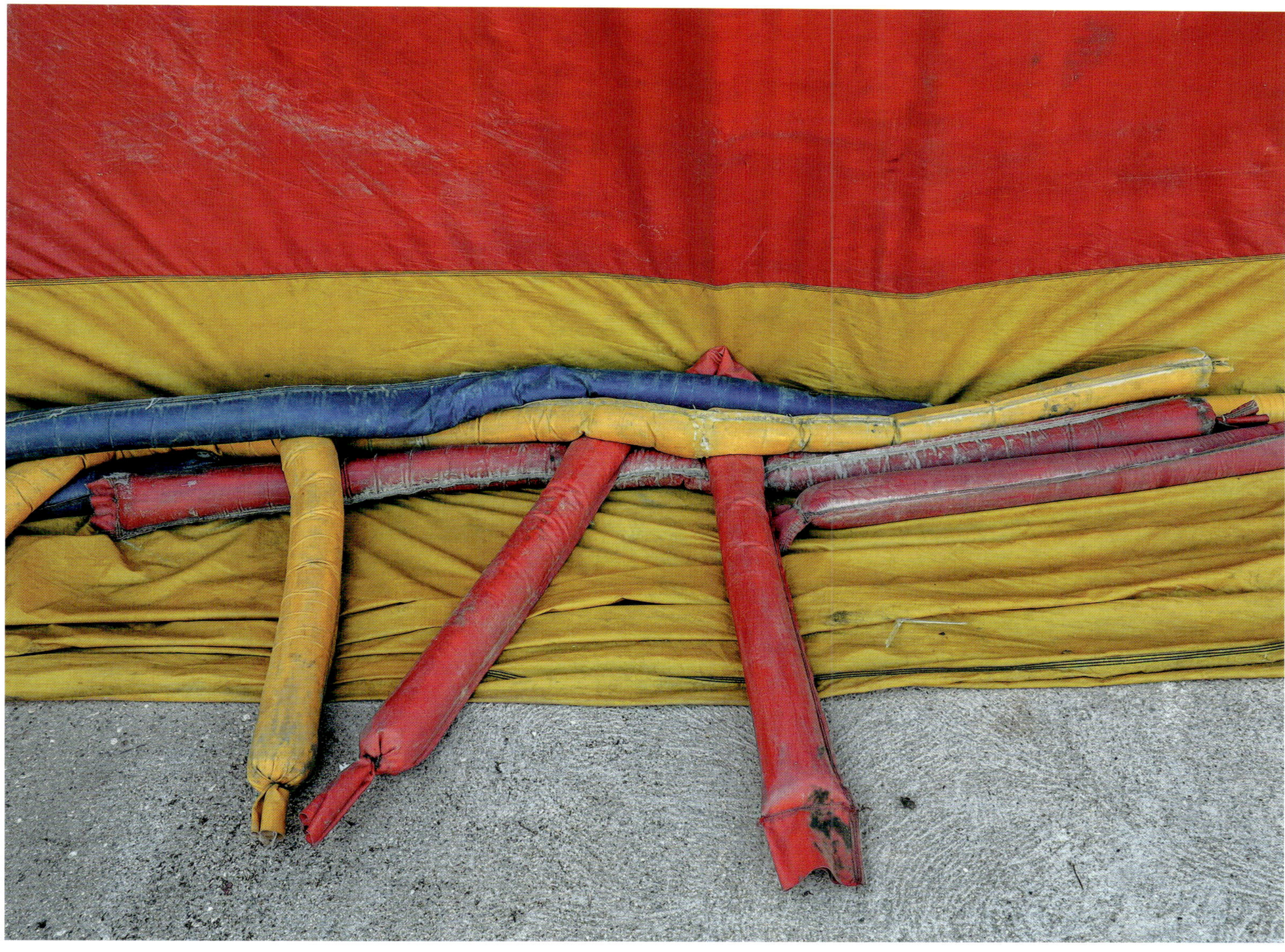

Ocean Front Walk

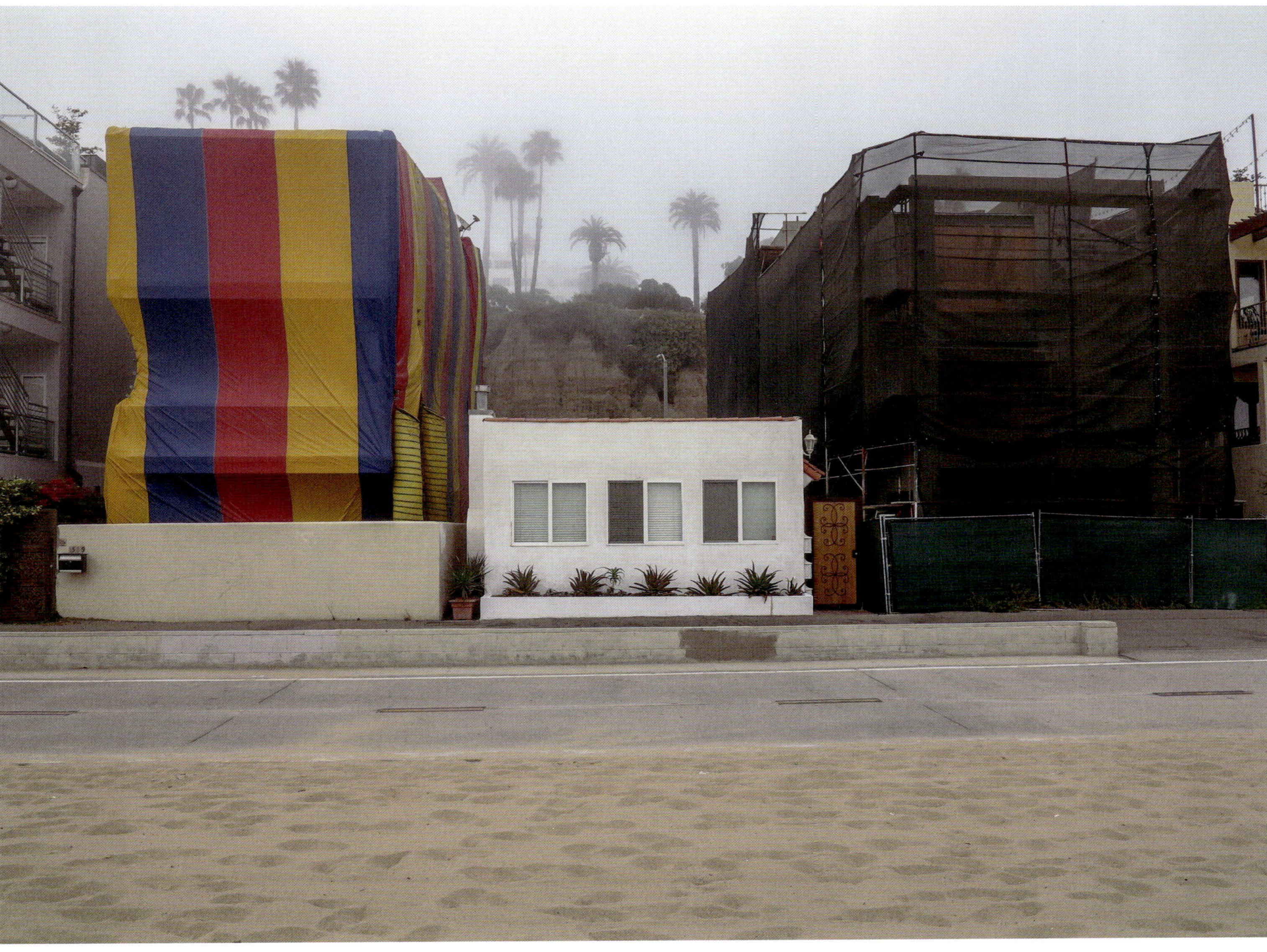

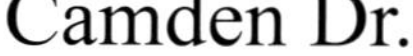
Camden Dr.

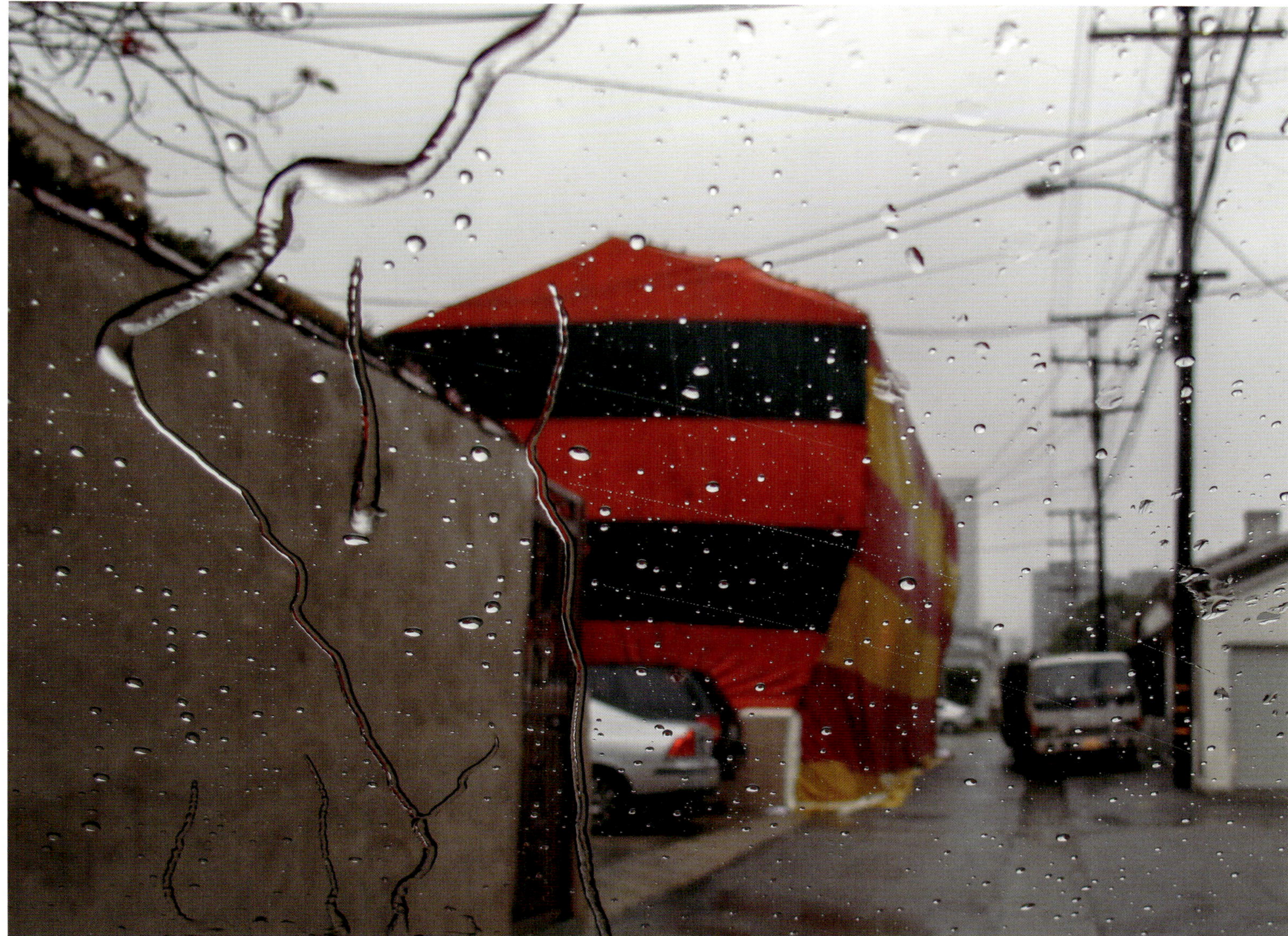

11th St.

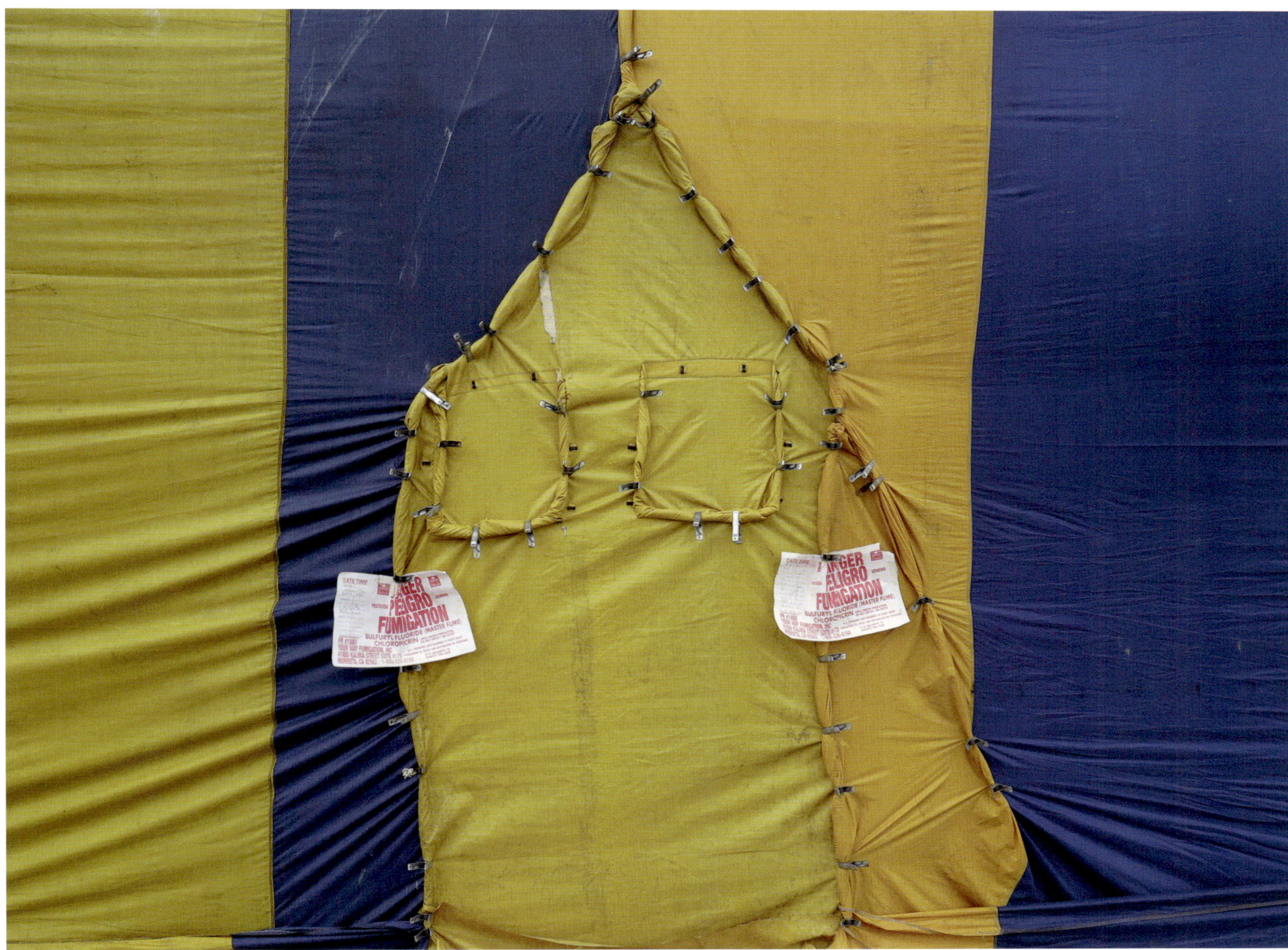
DATE TIME
VENENO
FUMIGATION
SULFURYL FLUORIDE (MASTER FUME)
CHLOROPICRIN
DATE TIME
FUMIGATION
SULFURYL FLUORIDE (MASTER FUME)
CHLOROPICRIN

Mindanao Way

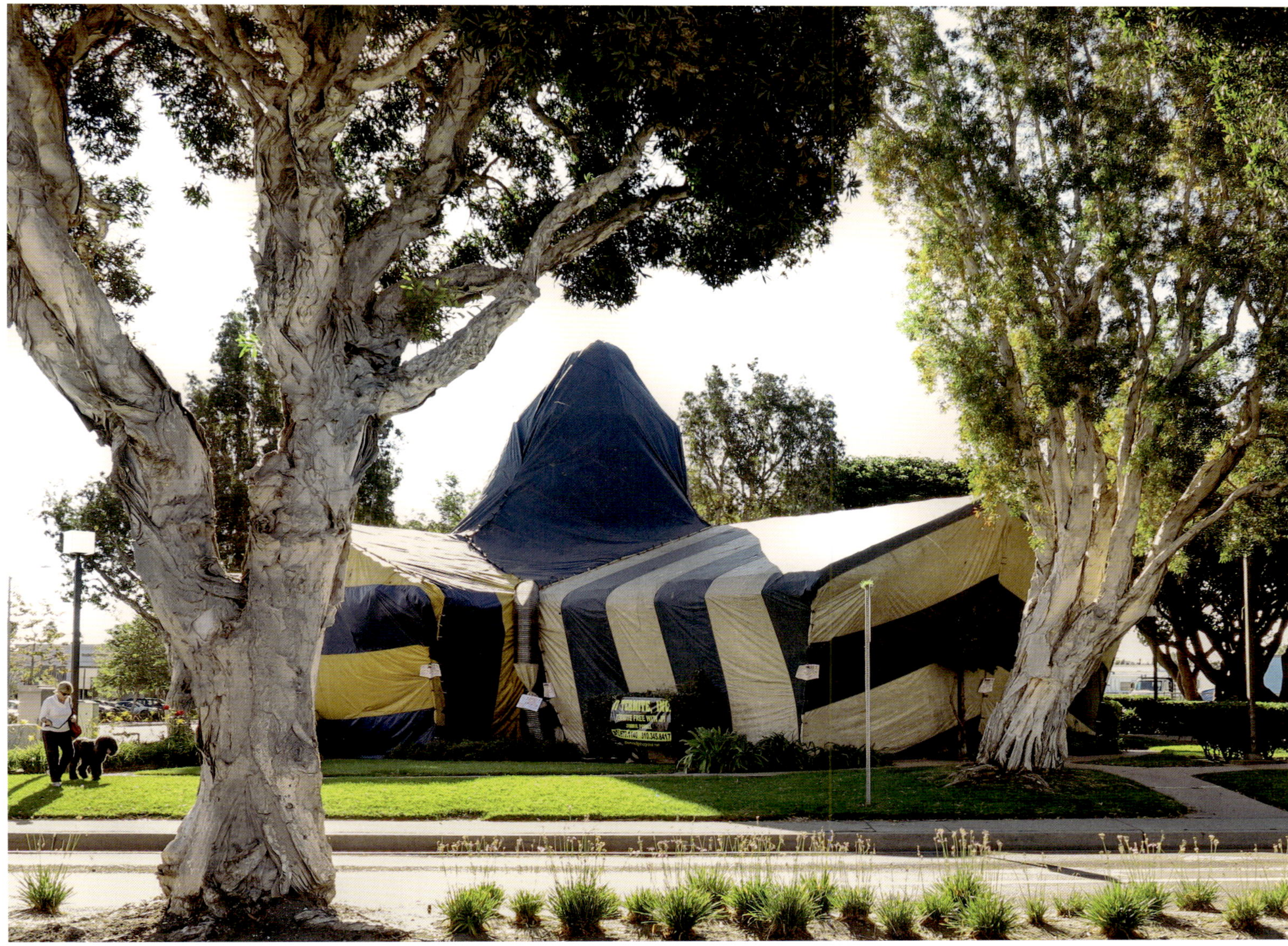
310.345.8417

Morningside Way

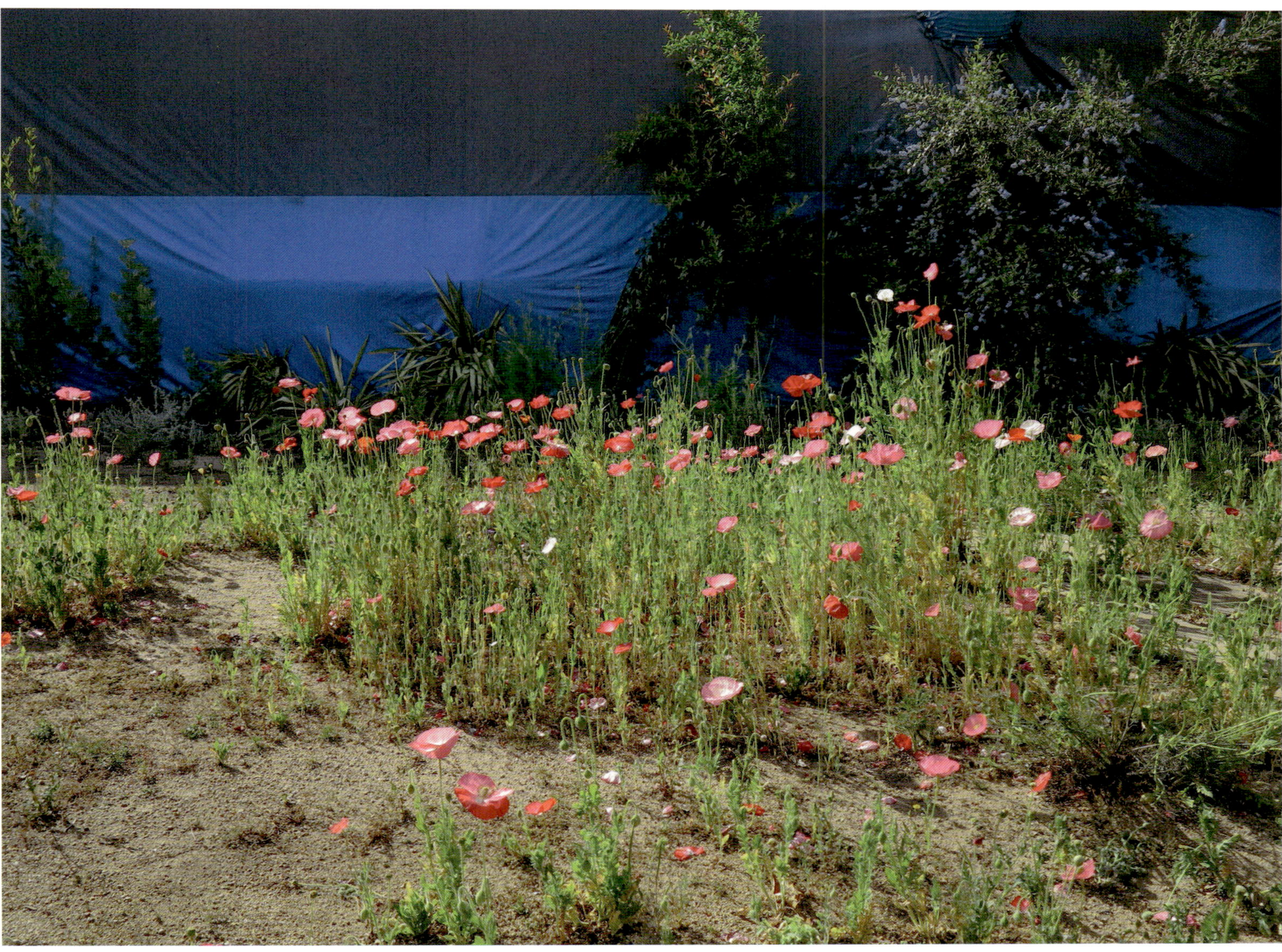

Berkeley St.

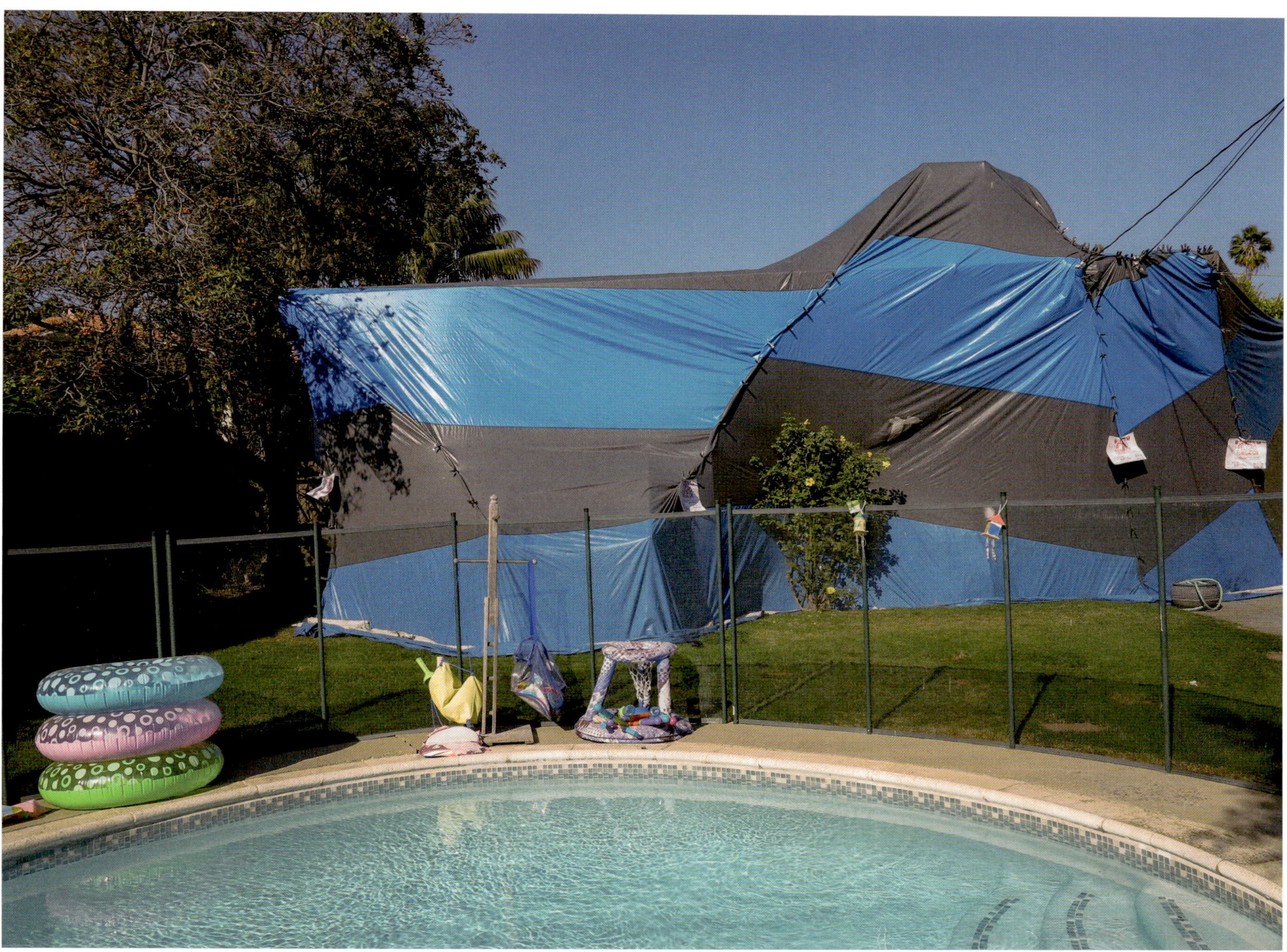

Pacific Coast Highway

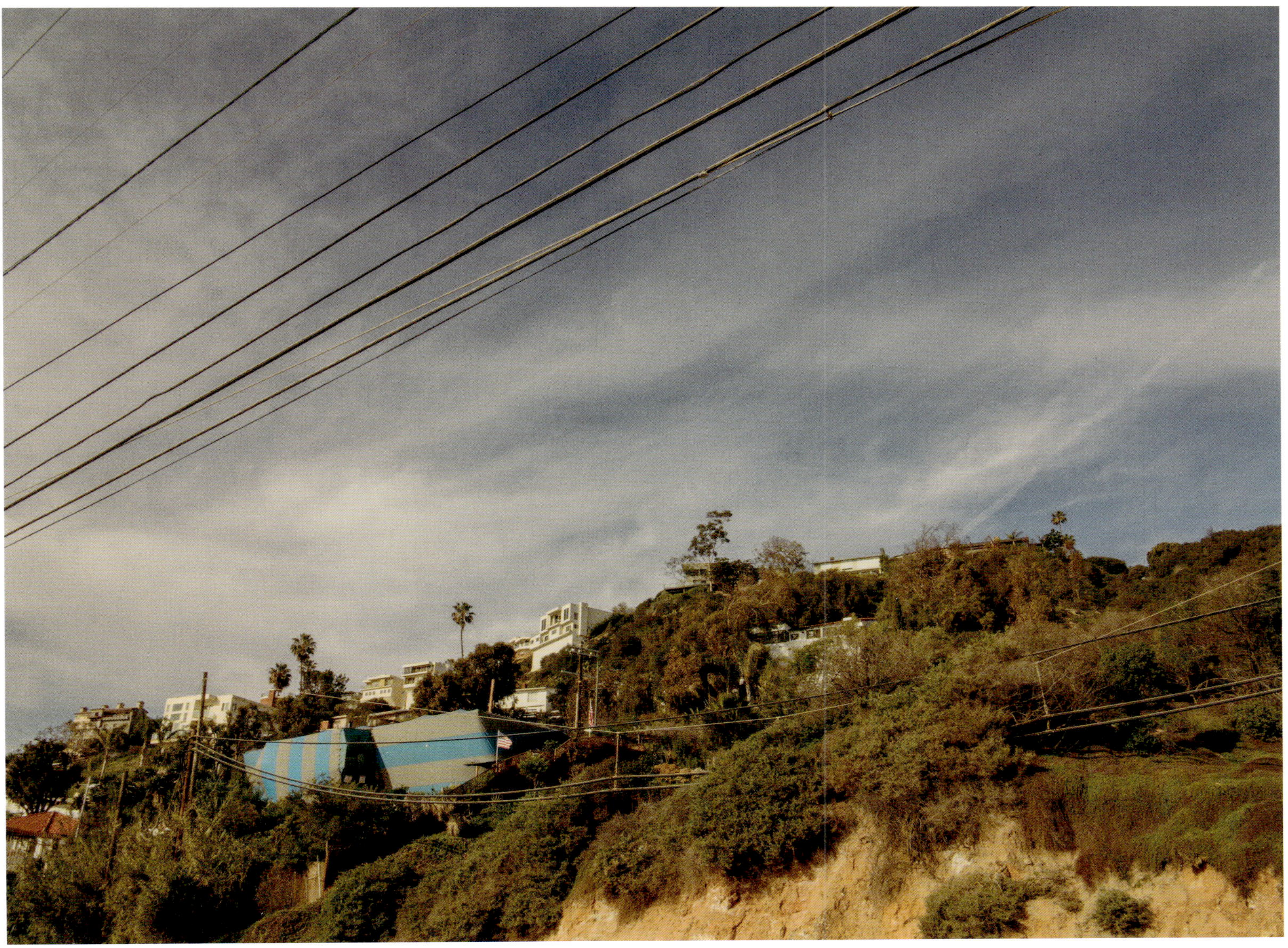

9th St.

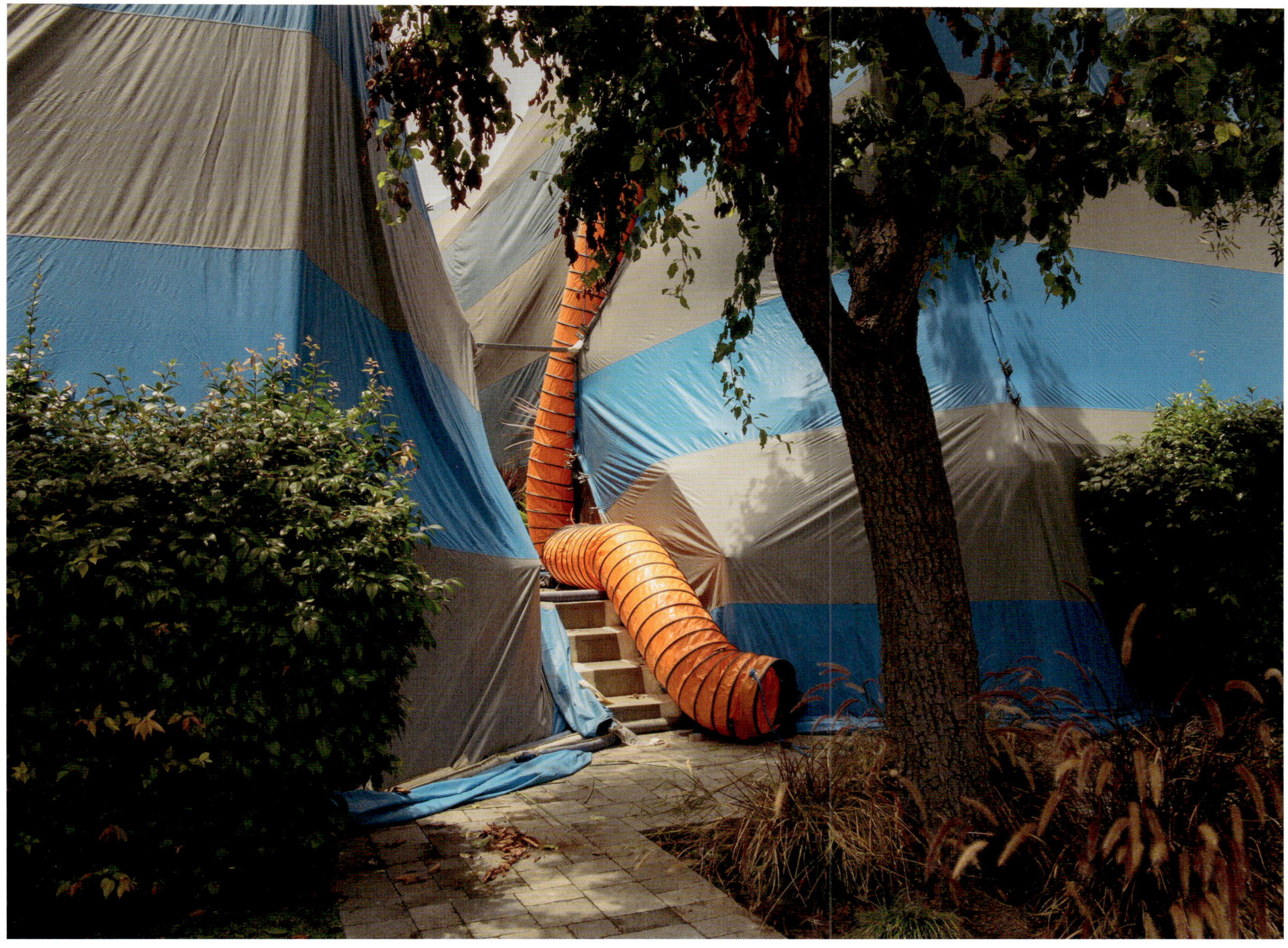

Westgate Ave.

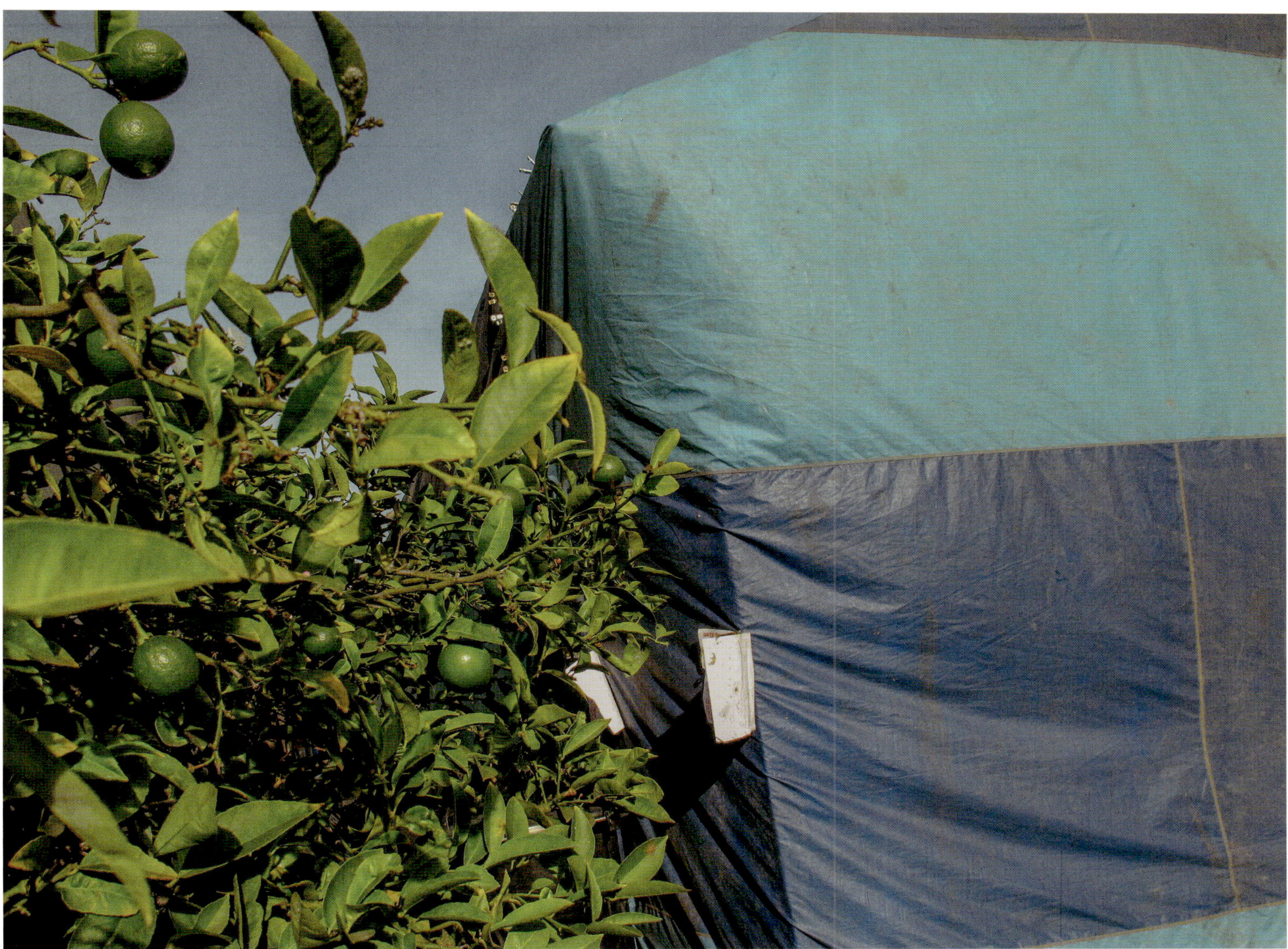

Caswell Ave.

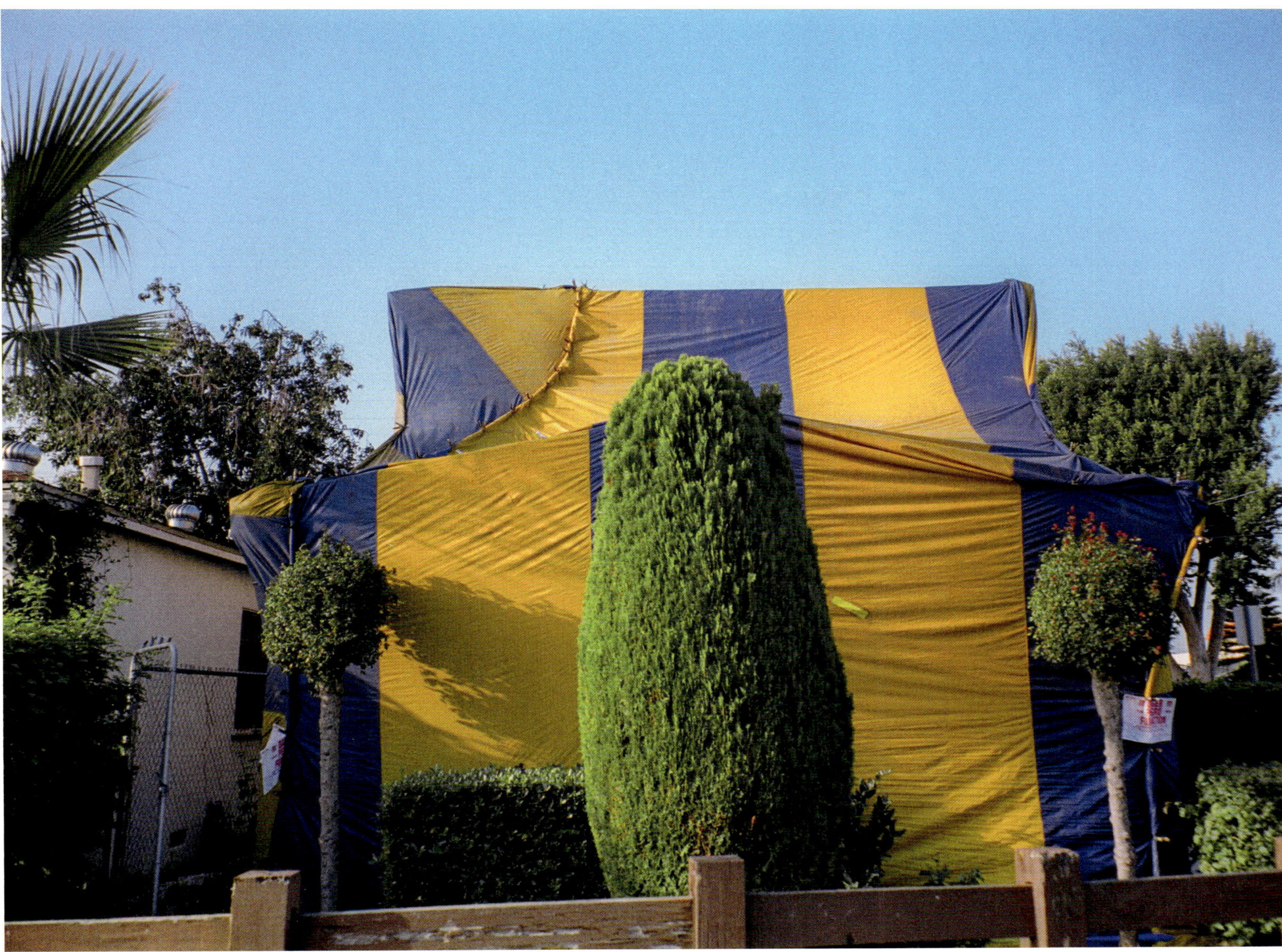

Pacific Coast Highway

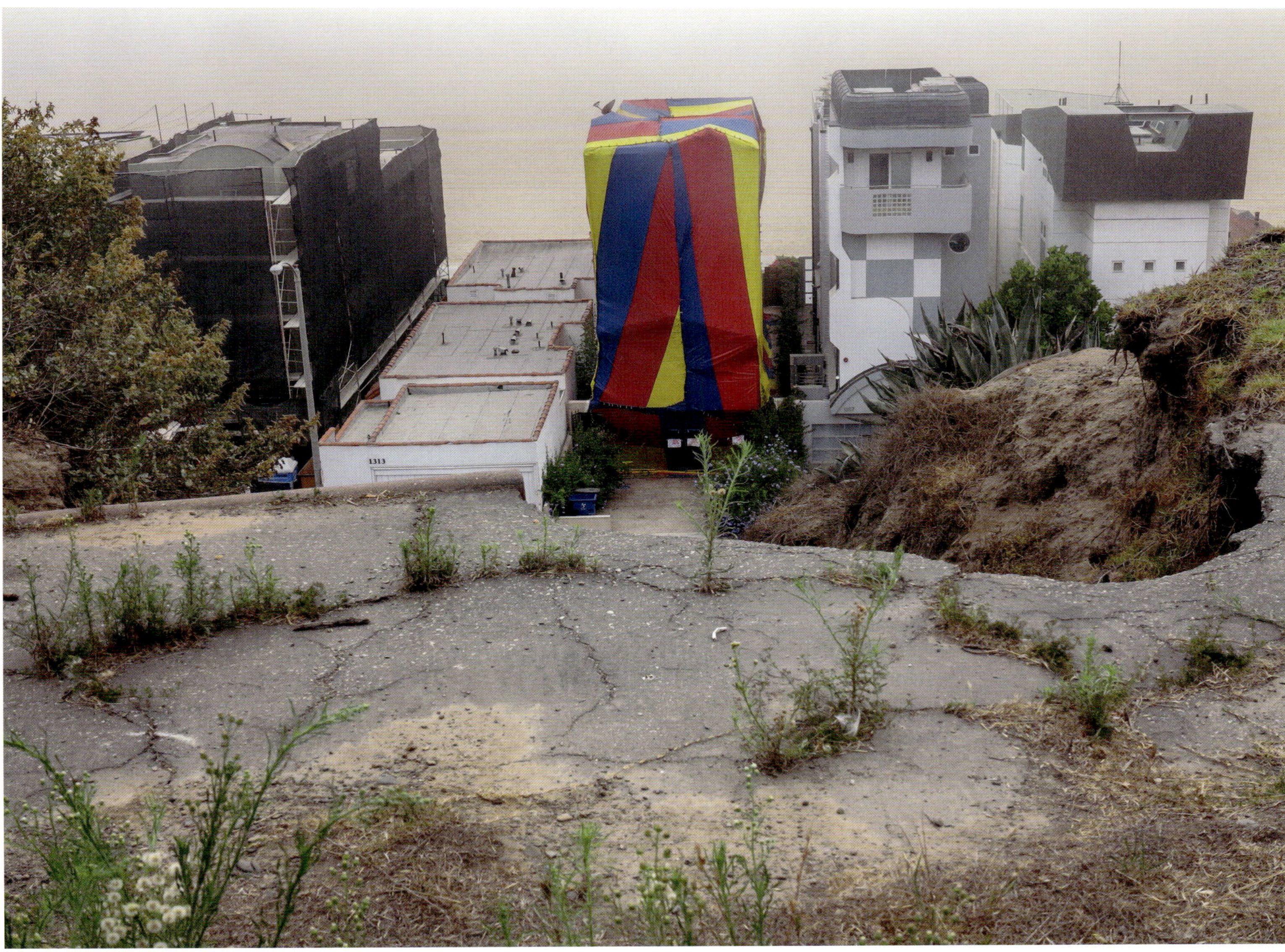
1313

Butler Ave.

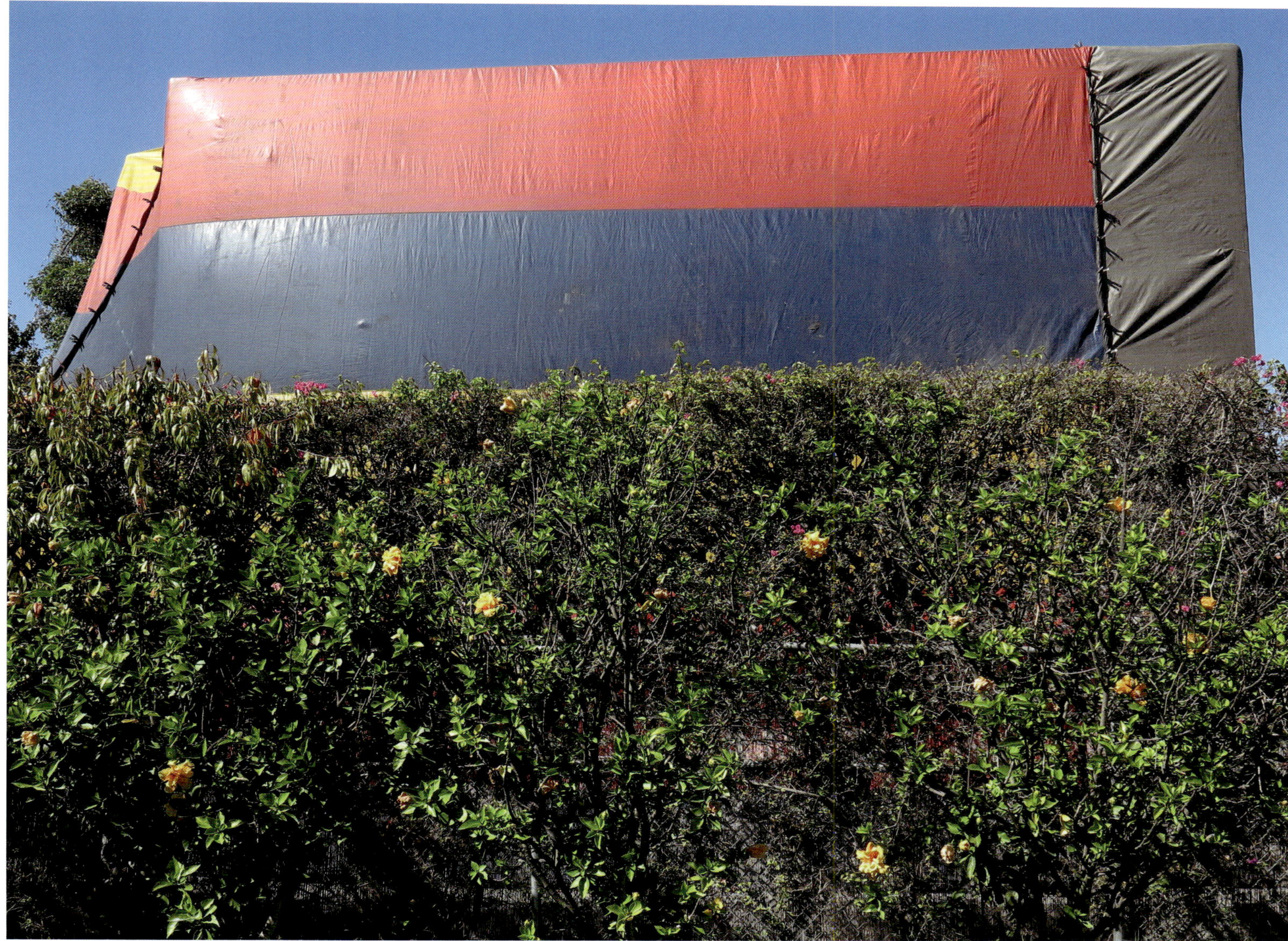

Chelsea Ave.

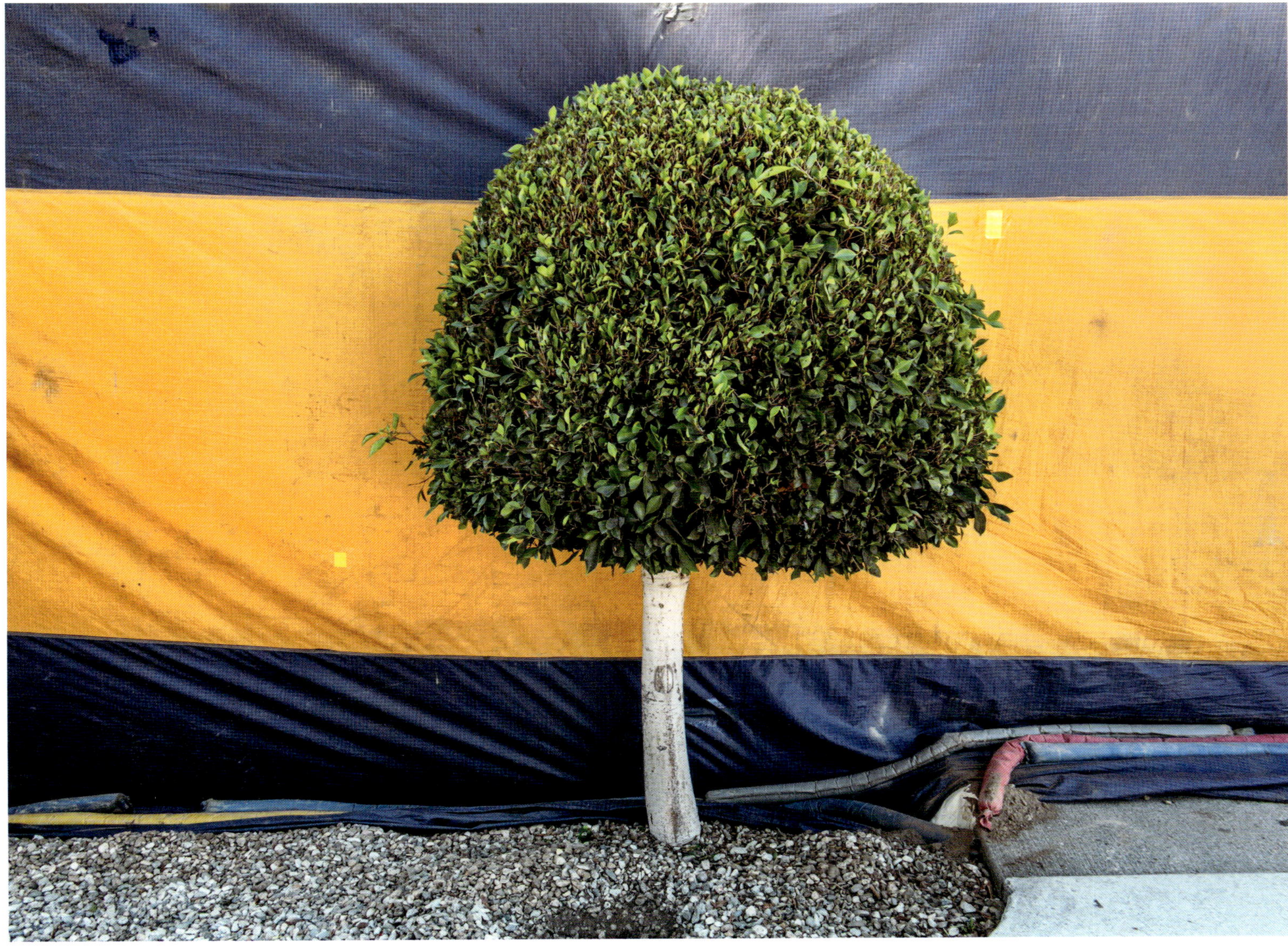

Bowling Green Way

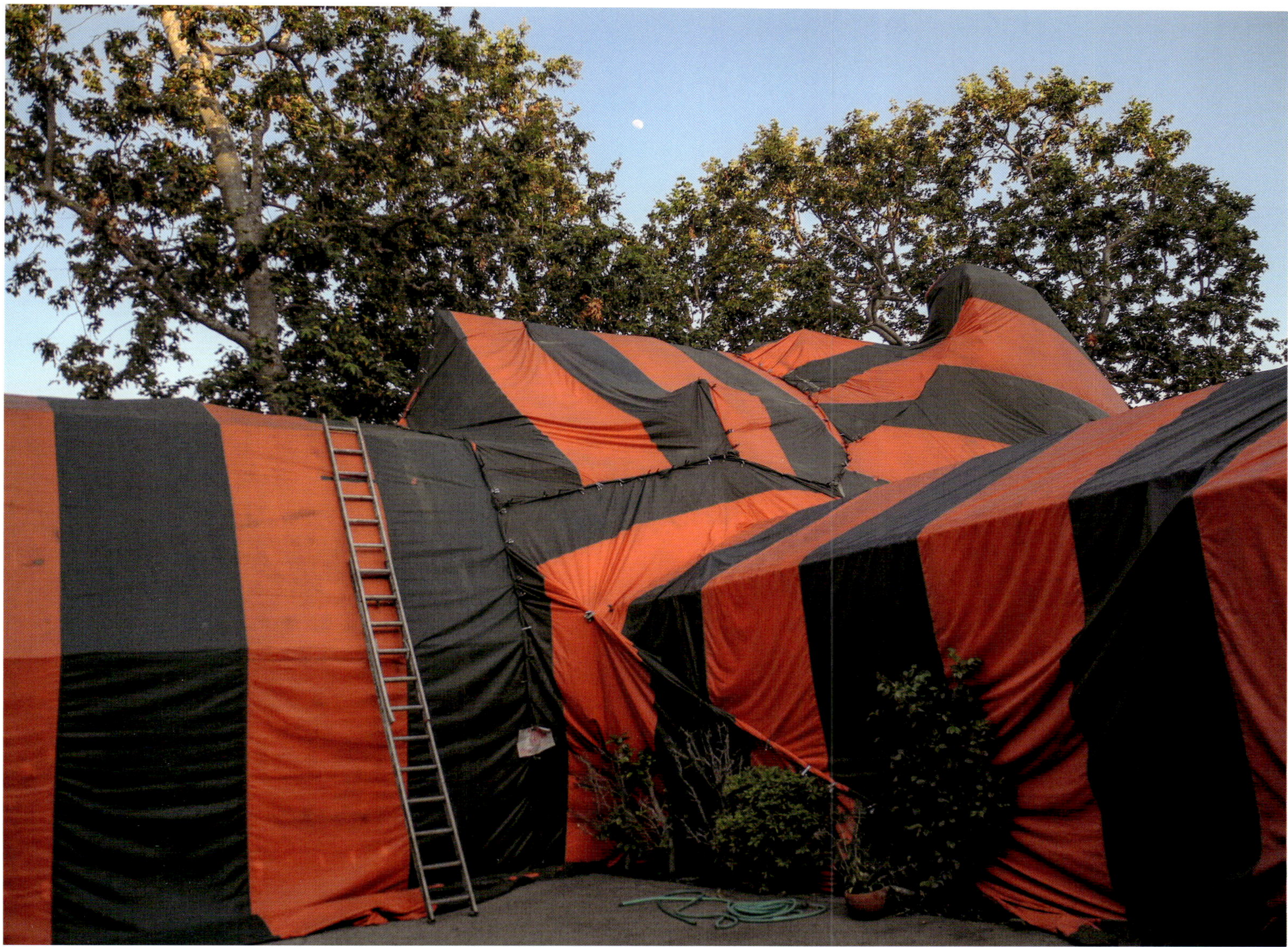

Montana Ave.

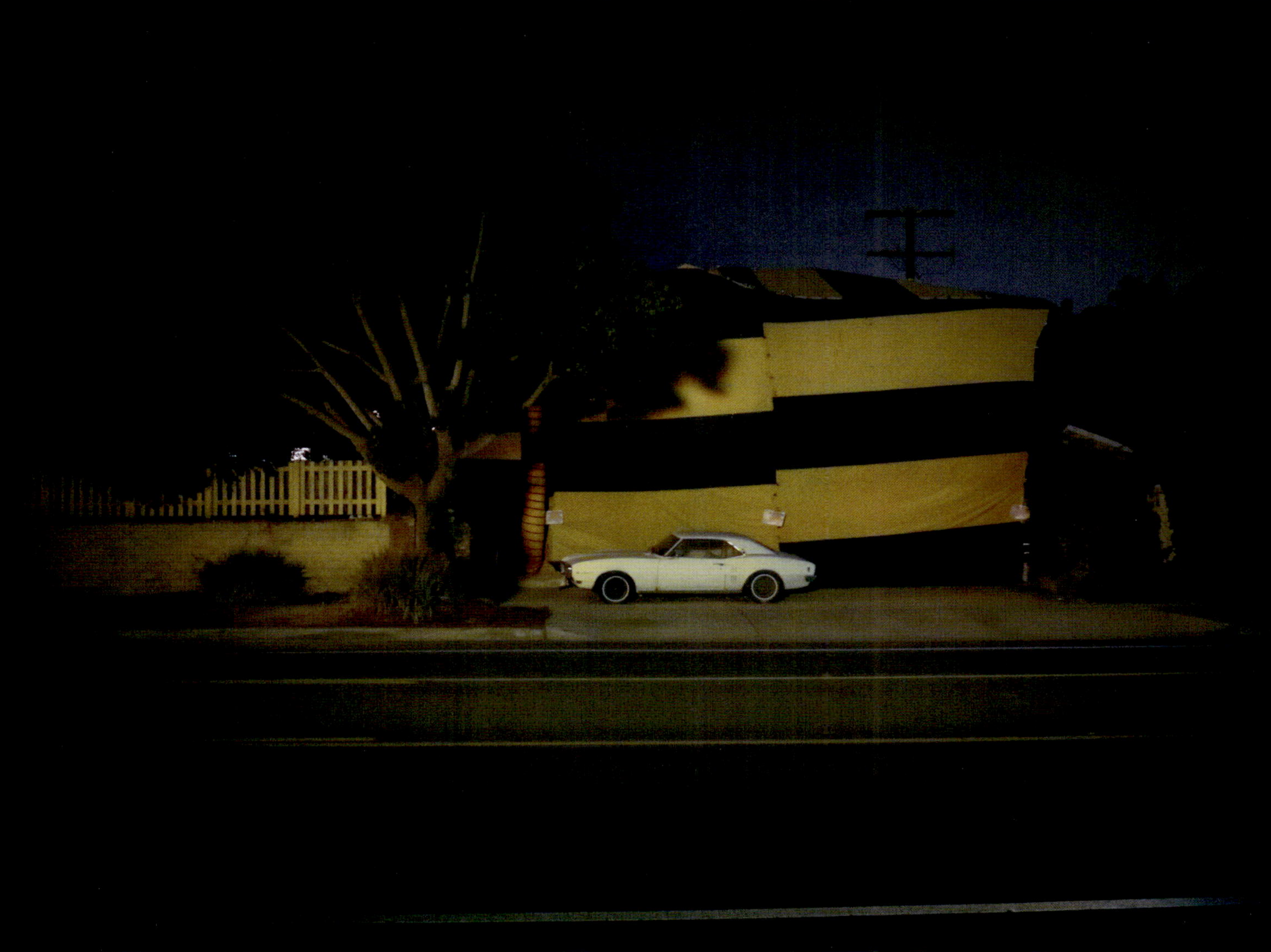

Admiralty Way

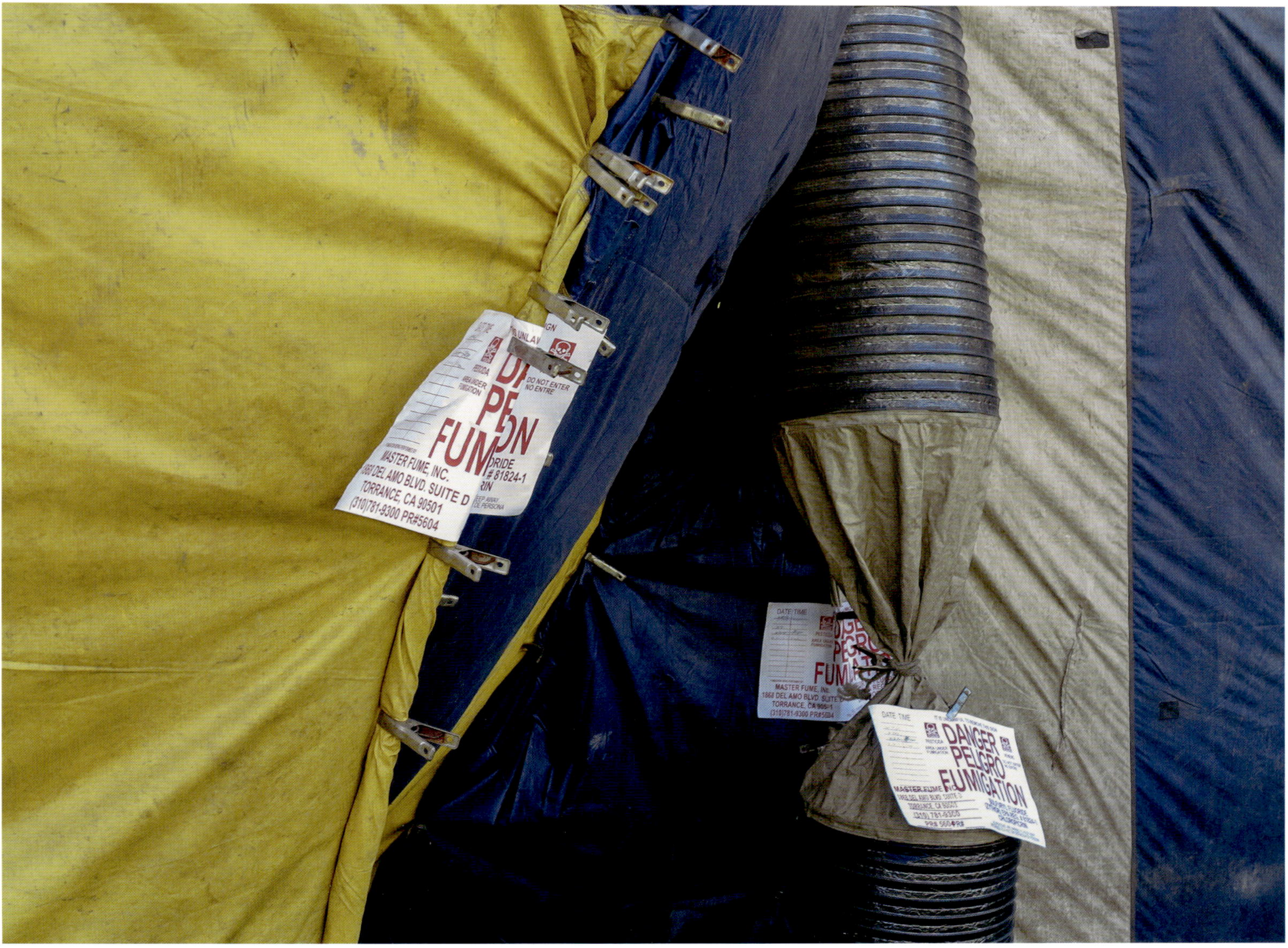
DO NOT ENTER
NO ENTRE
MASTER FUME, INC.
1868 DEL AMO BLVD. SUITE D
TORRANCE, CA 90501
(310)781-9300 PR#5604
DATE TIME
DATE TIME
DANGER
PELIGRO
FUMIGATION

Ocean Front Walk

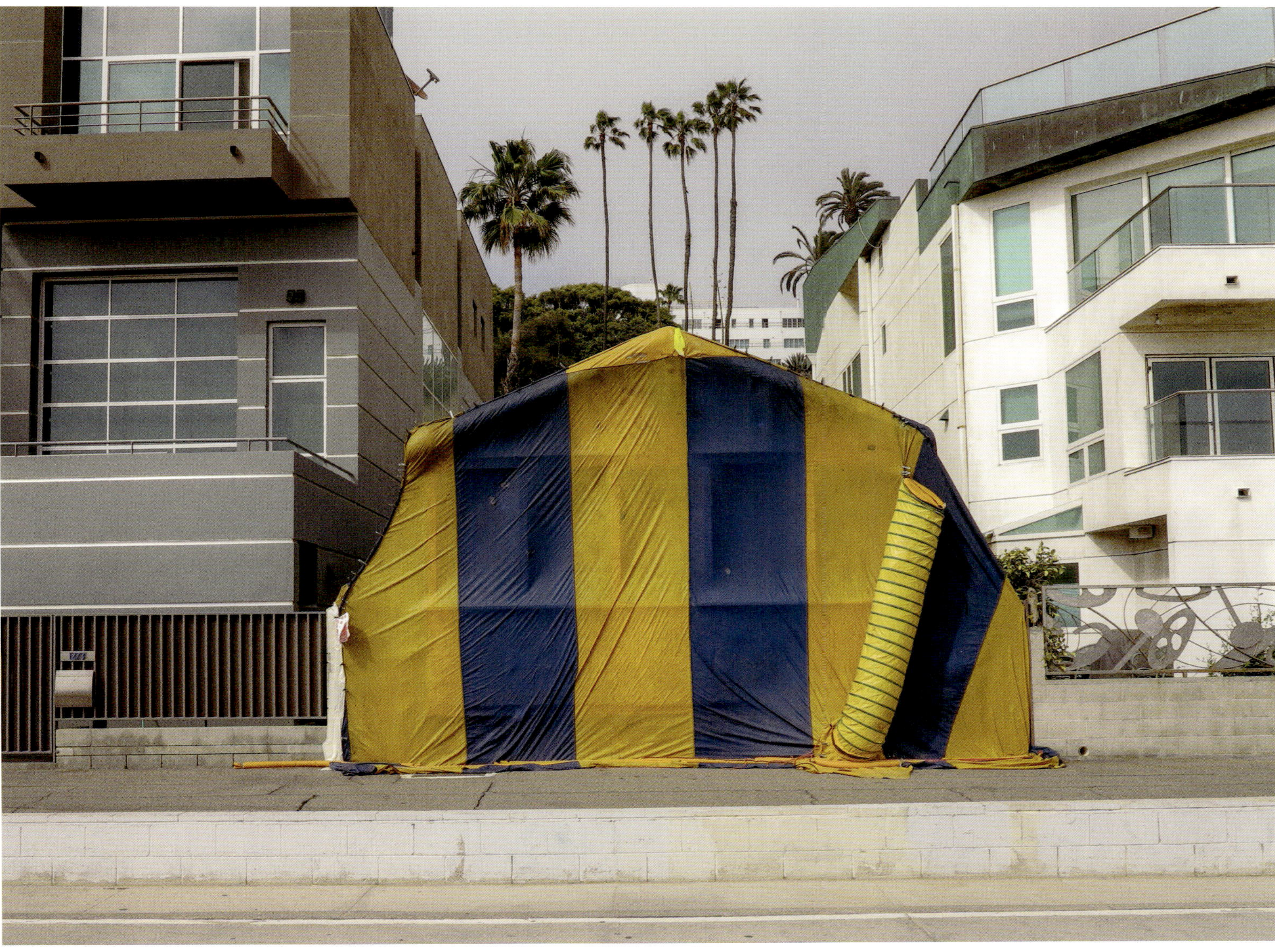

4th St.

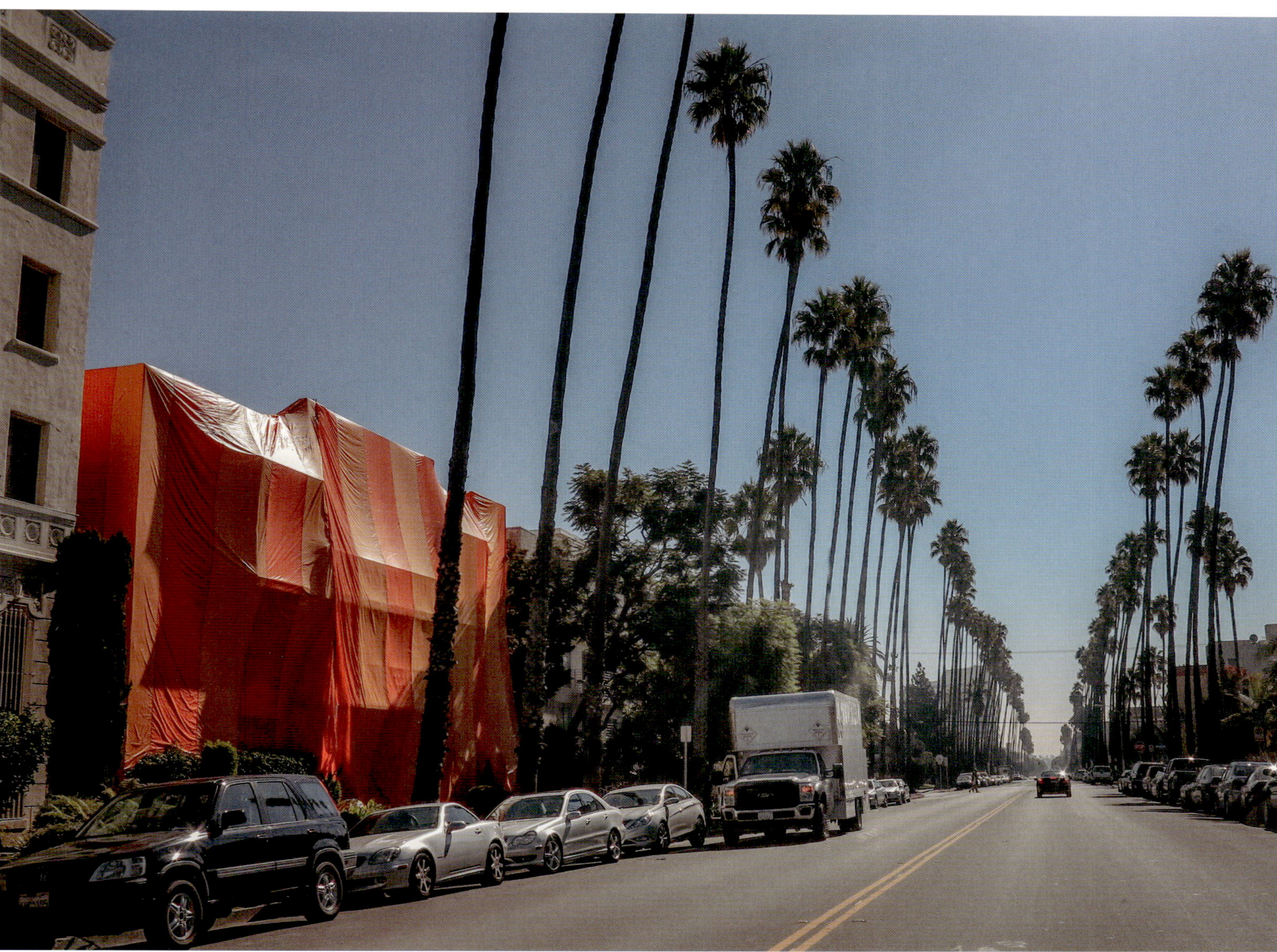

Santa Monica Blvd.

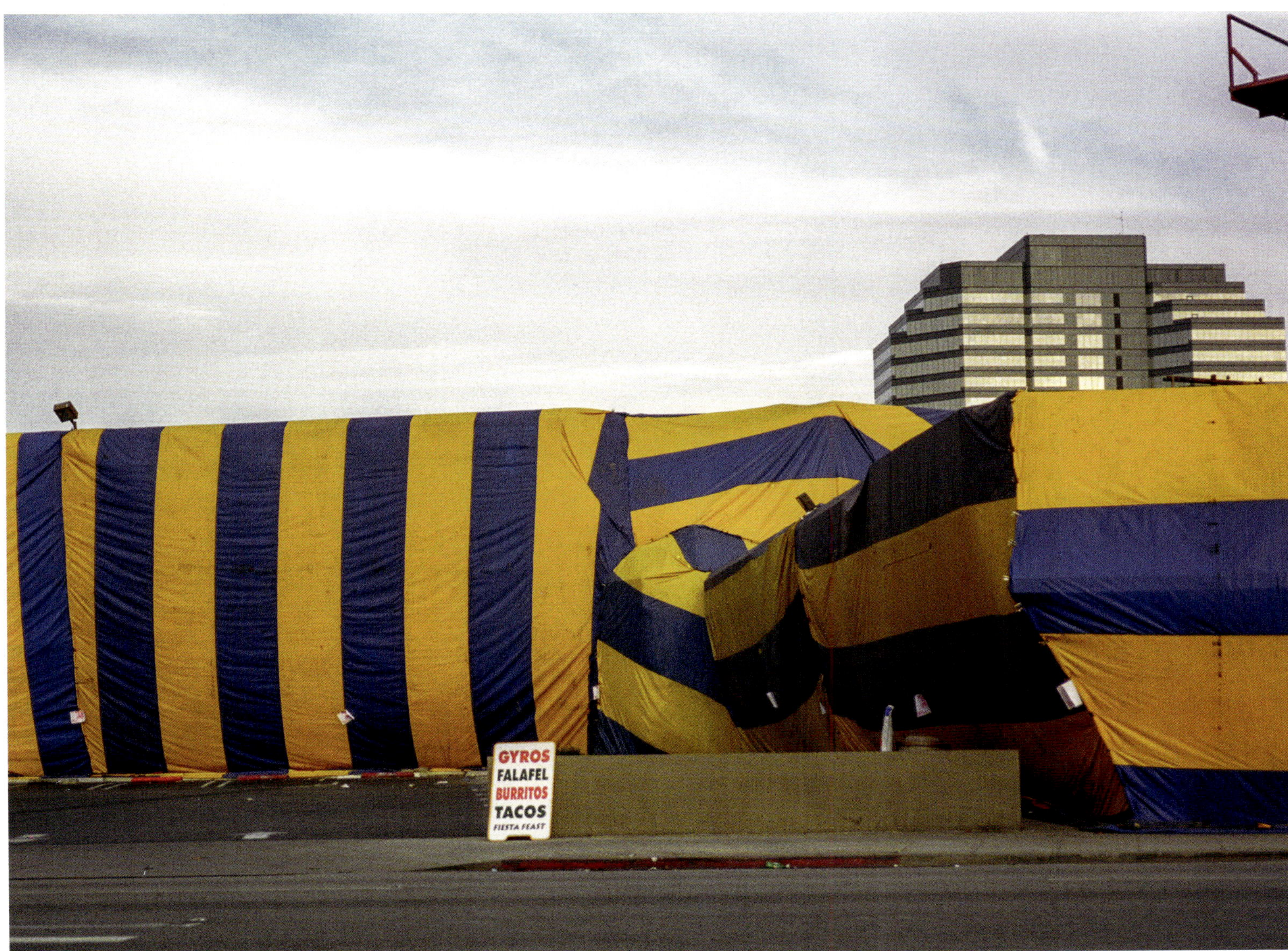
GYROS
FALAFEL
BURRITOS
TACOS
FIESTA FEAST

S Barrington Ave.

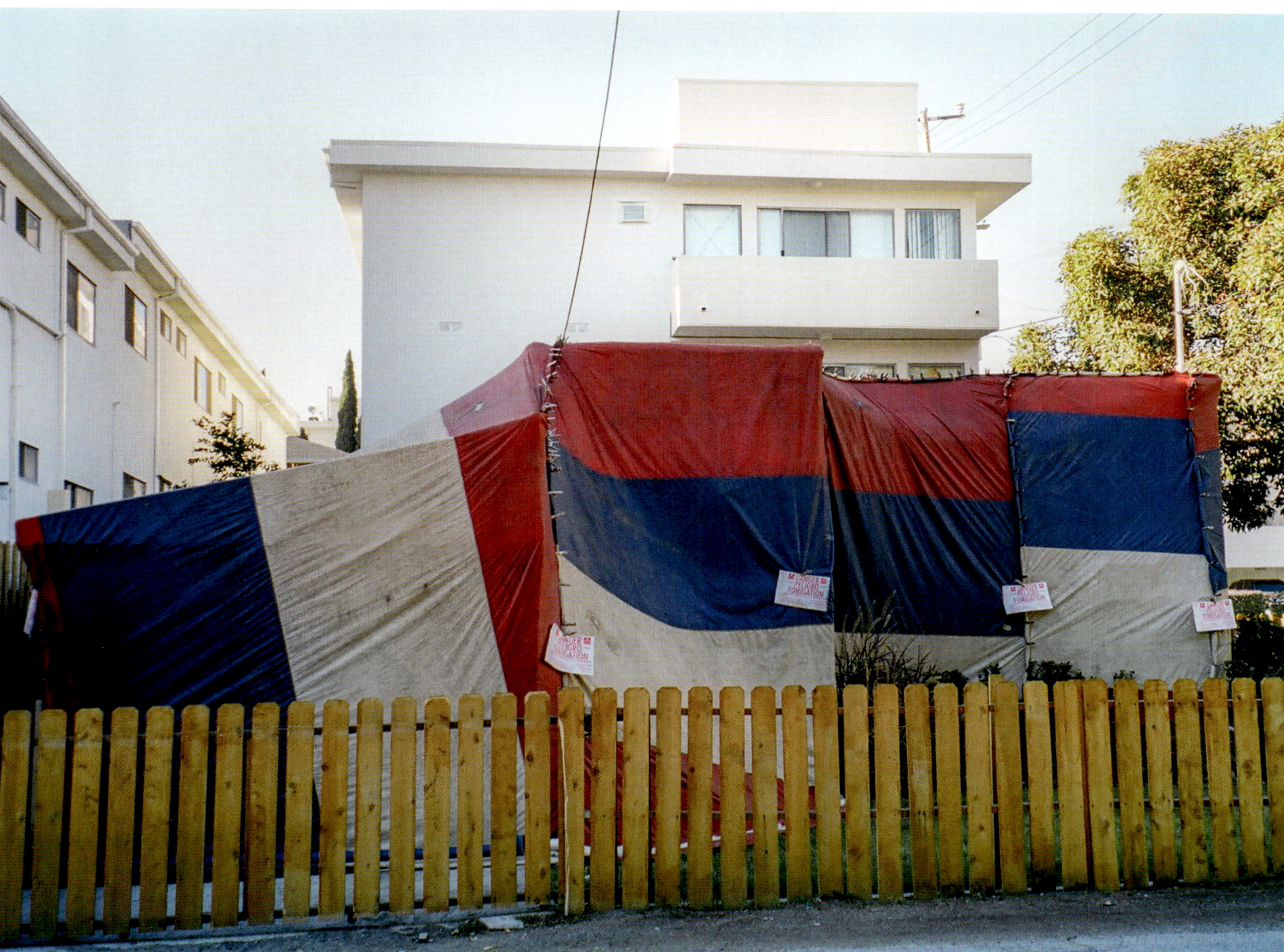
FUMIGATION

Admiralty Way

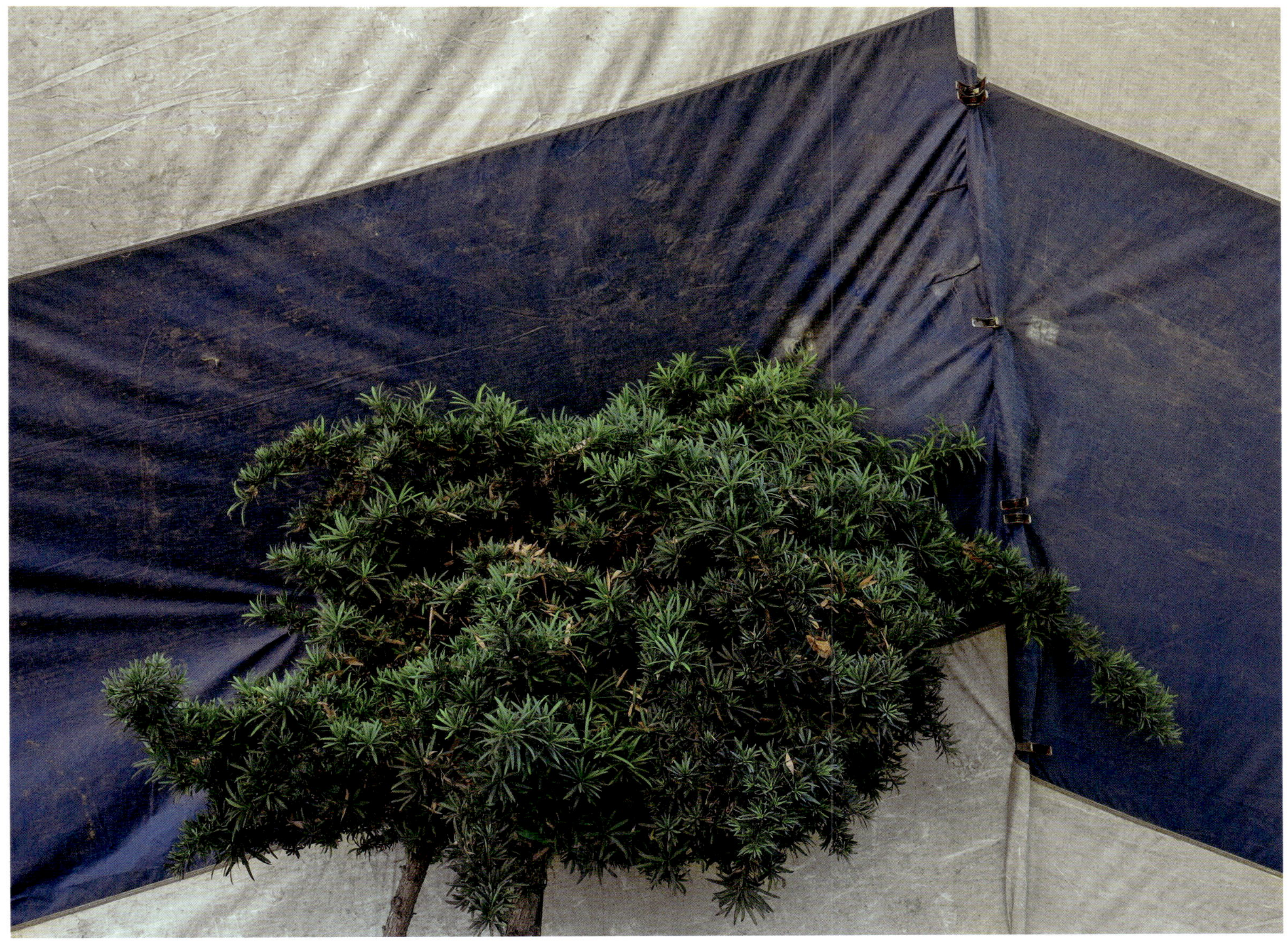

Penmar Ave.

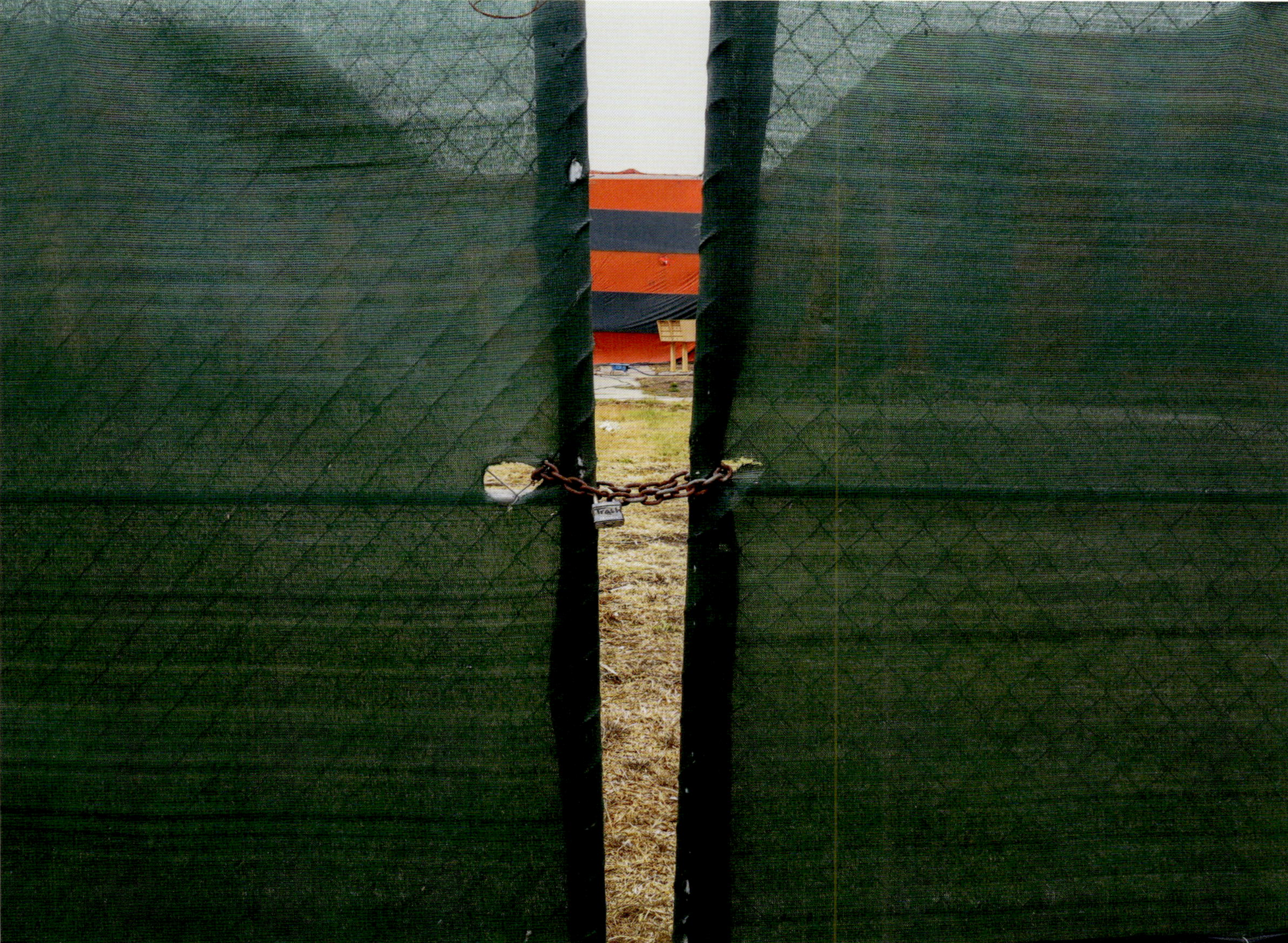

S Bristol Ave.

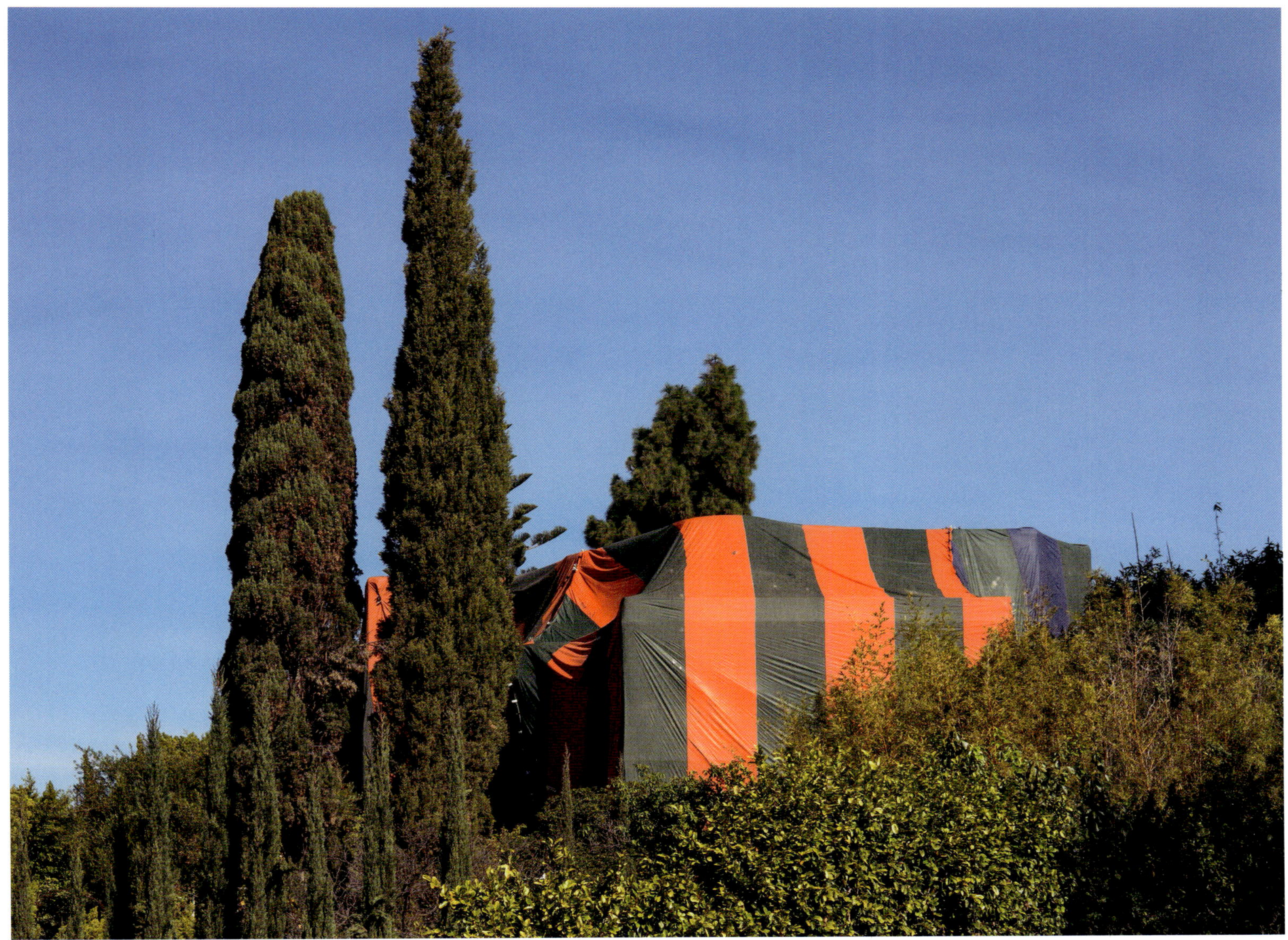

Lake St.

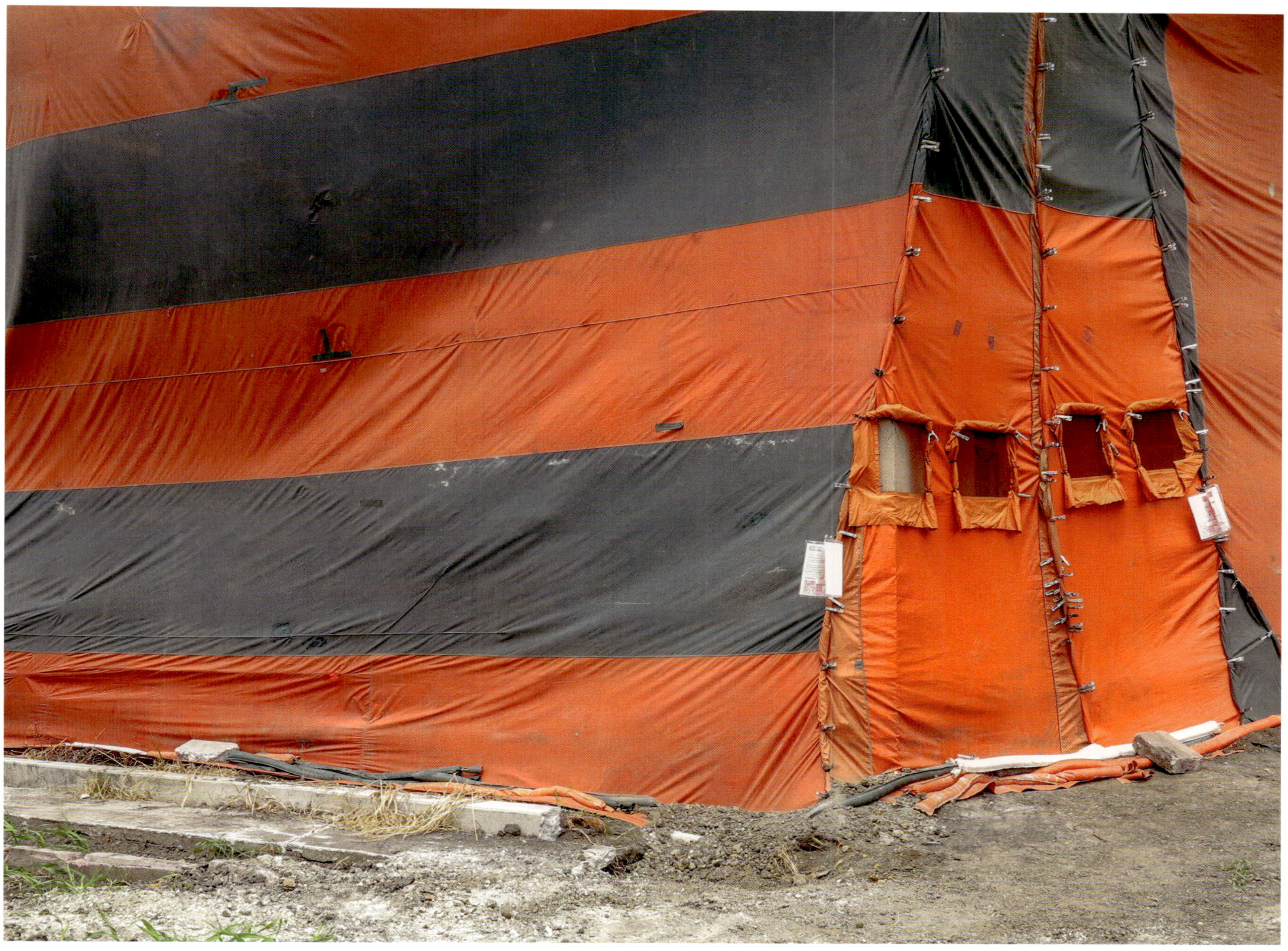

Venice Way

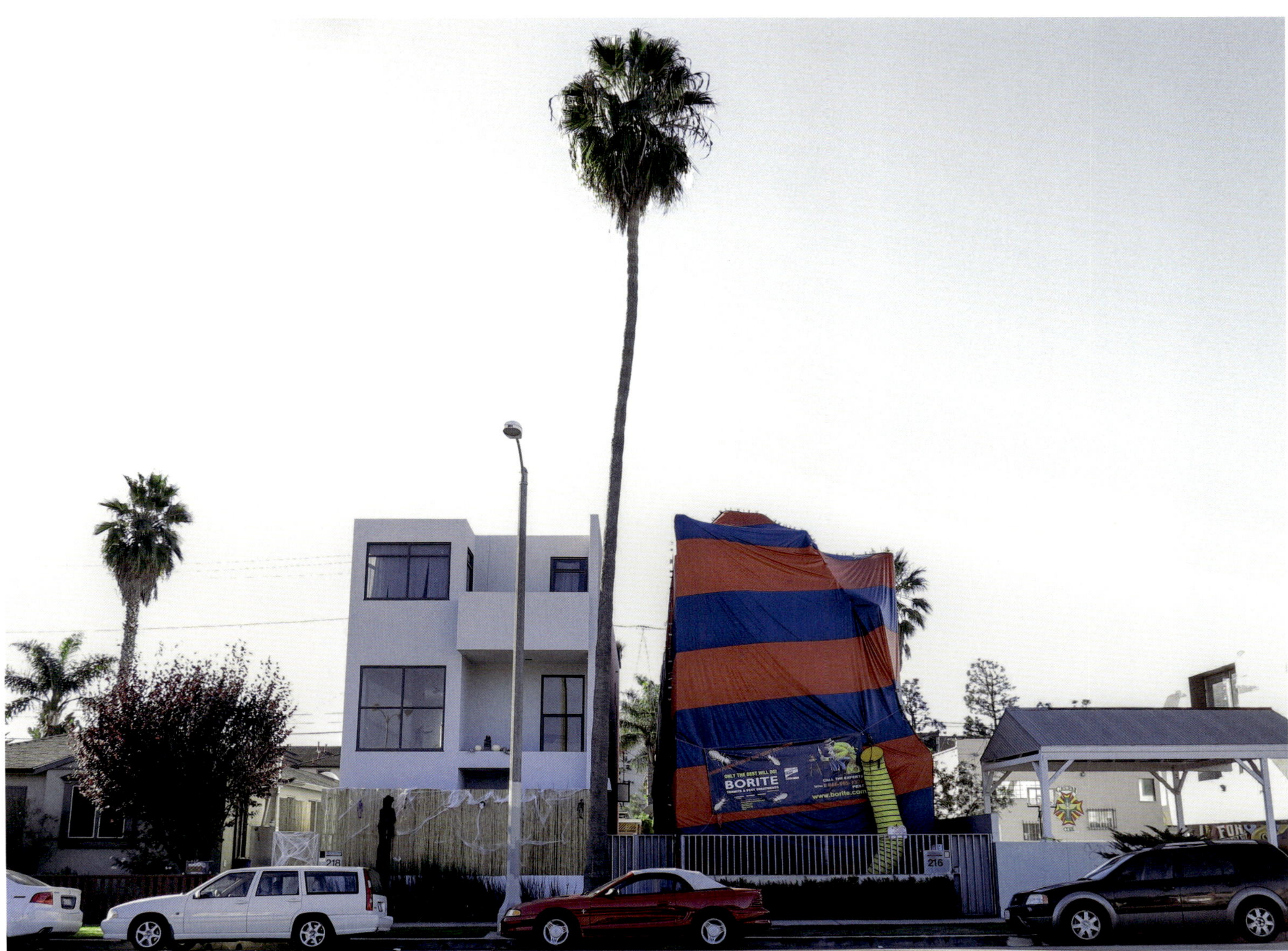
ONLY THE BEST WILL DO!
BORITE
TERMITE & PEST TREATMENTS
www.borite.com
218
216

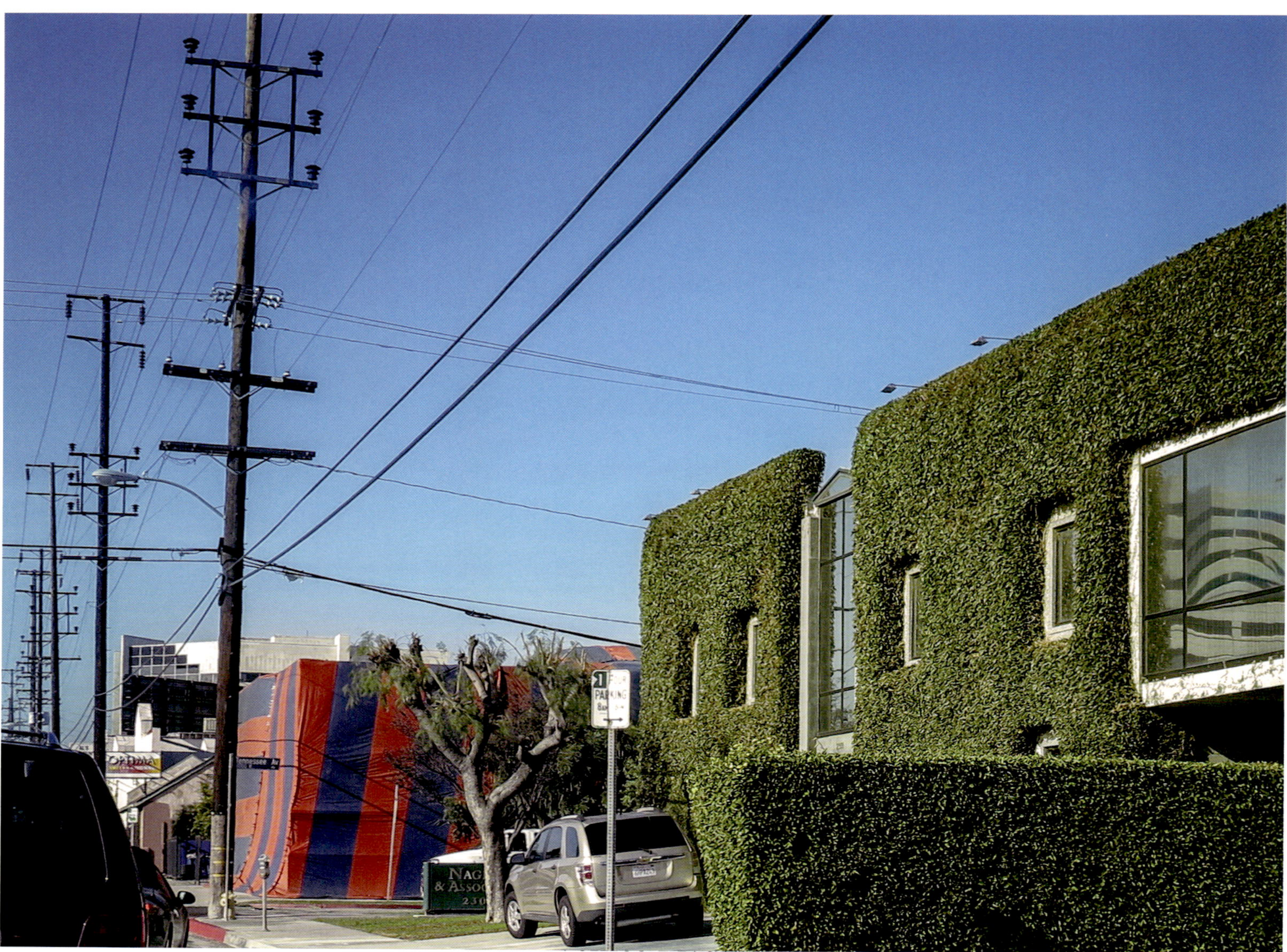
FOUR
PARKING

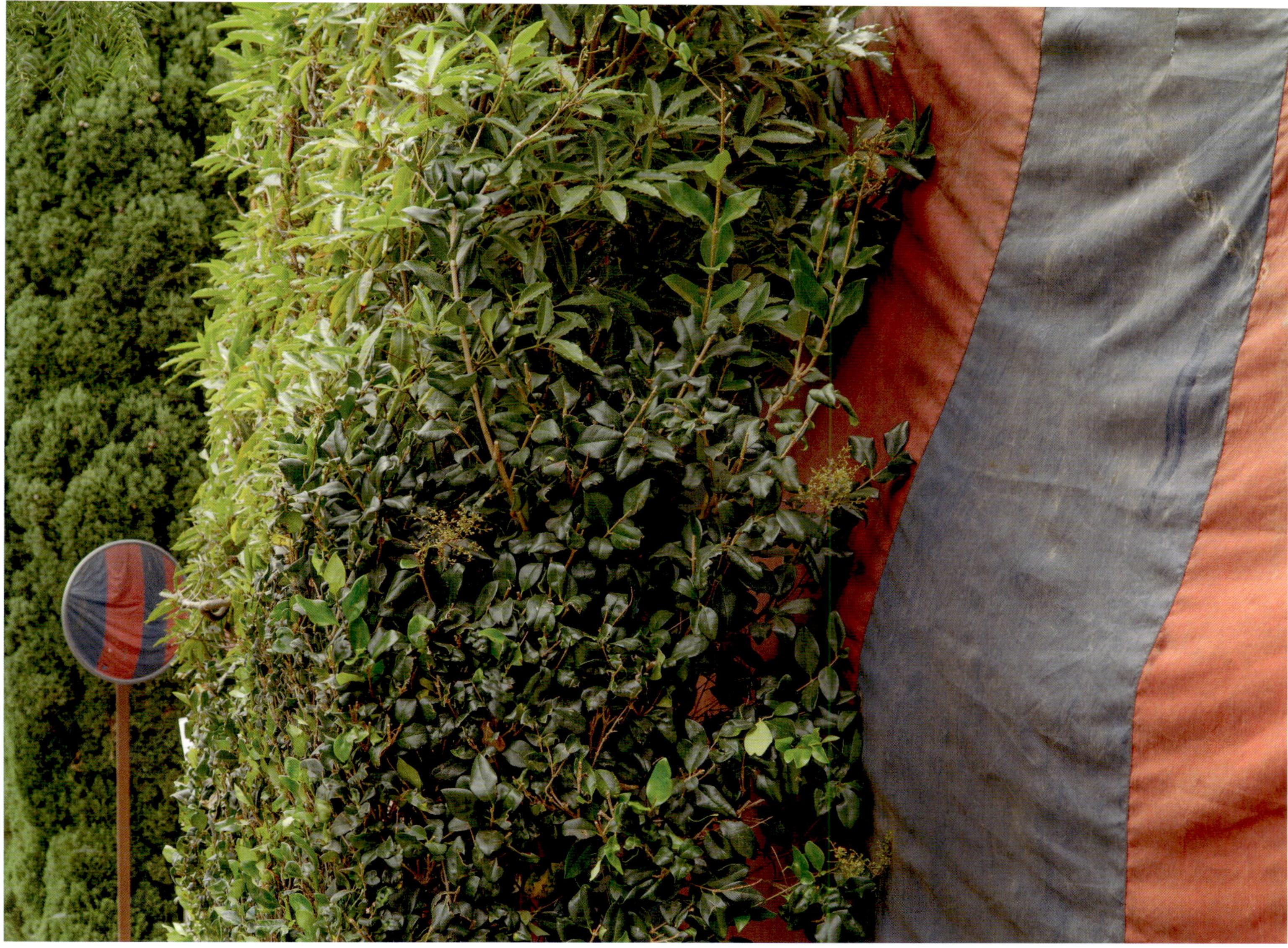

Hughes Ave.

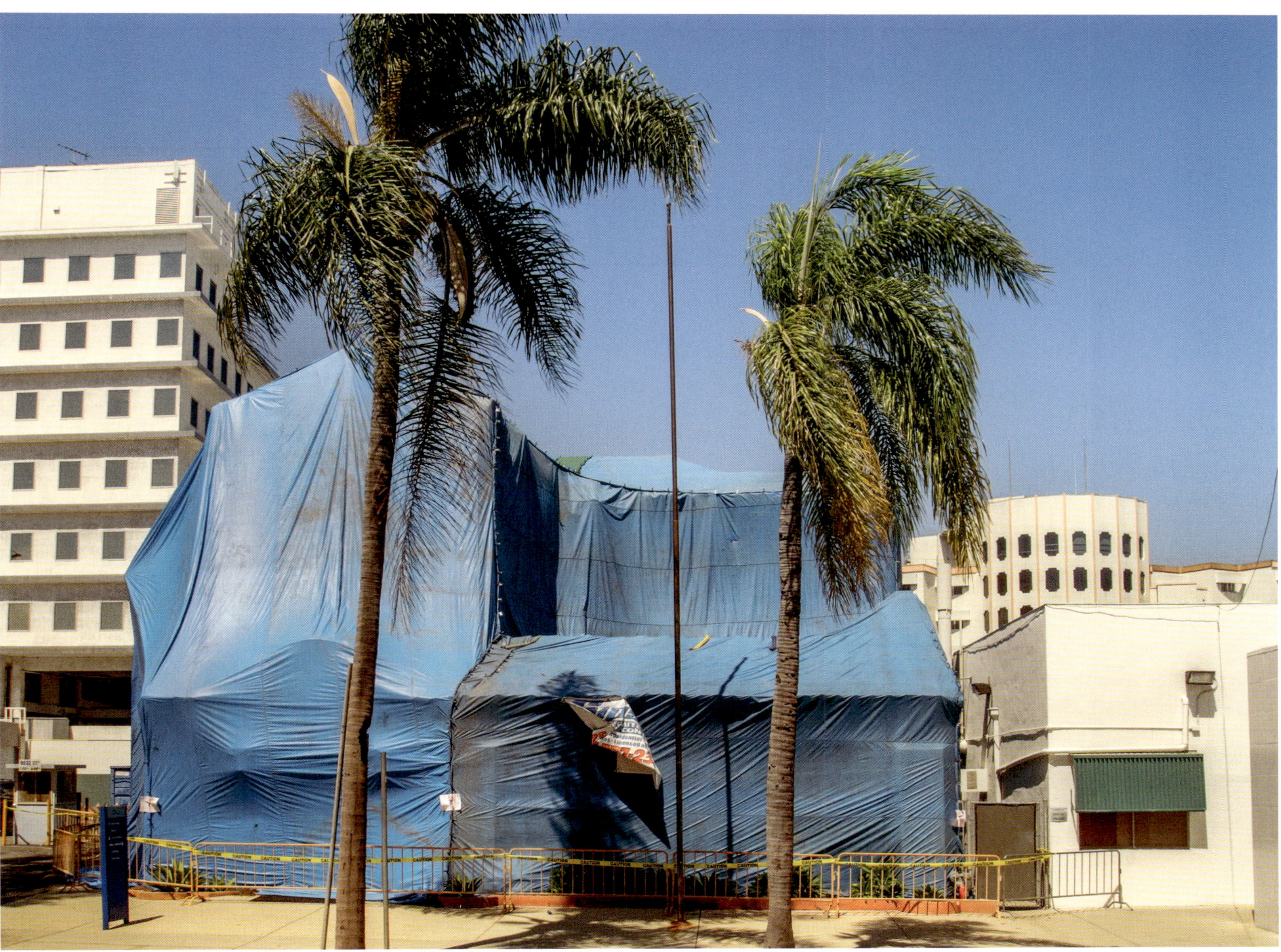

Allenford Ave.

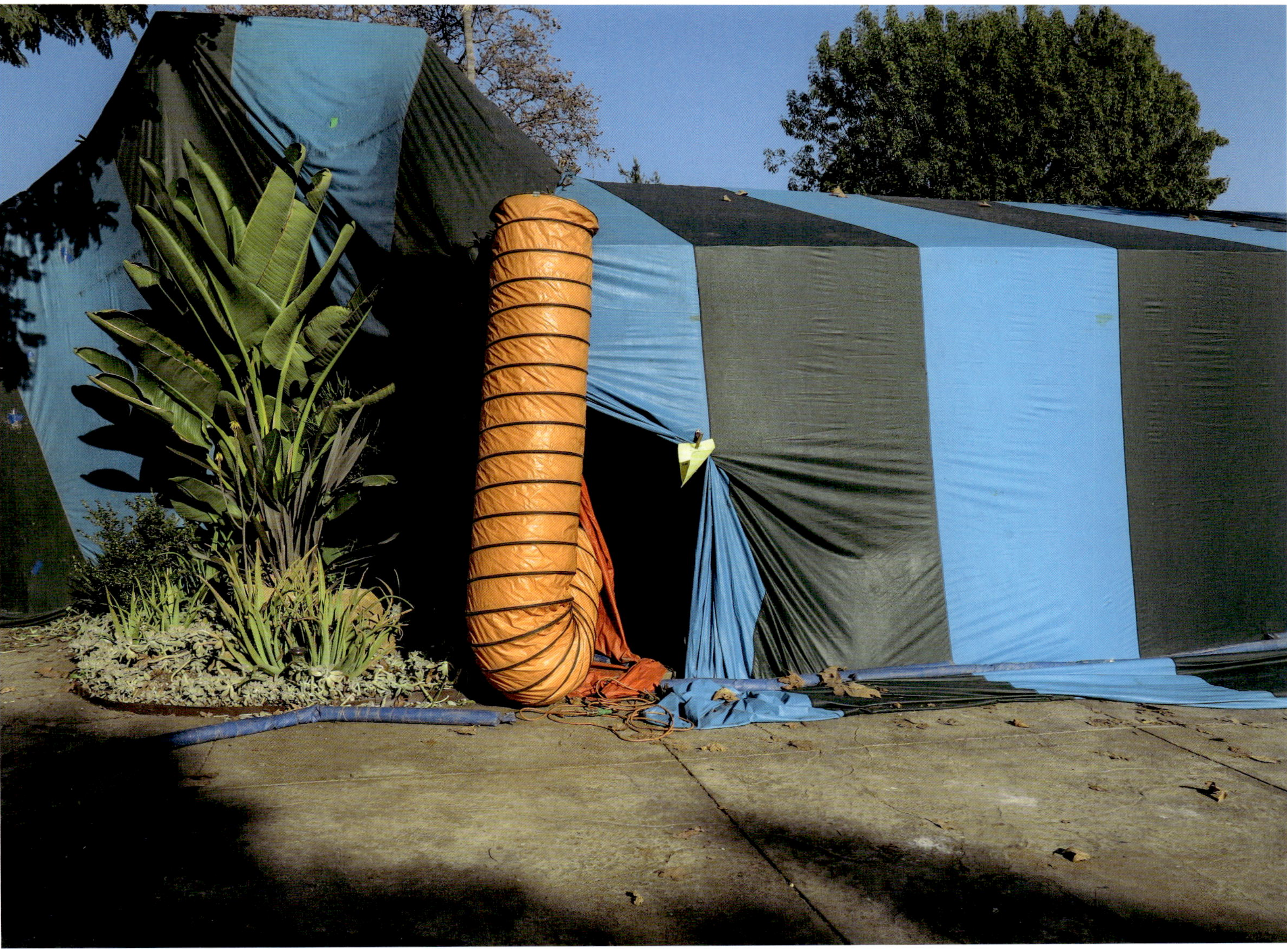

Pontoon Pl.

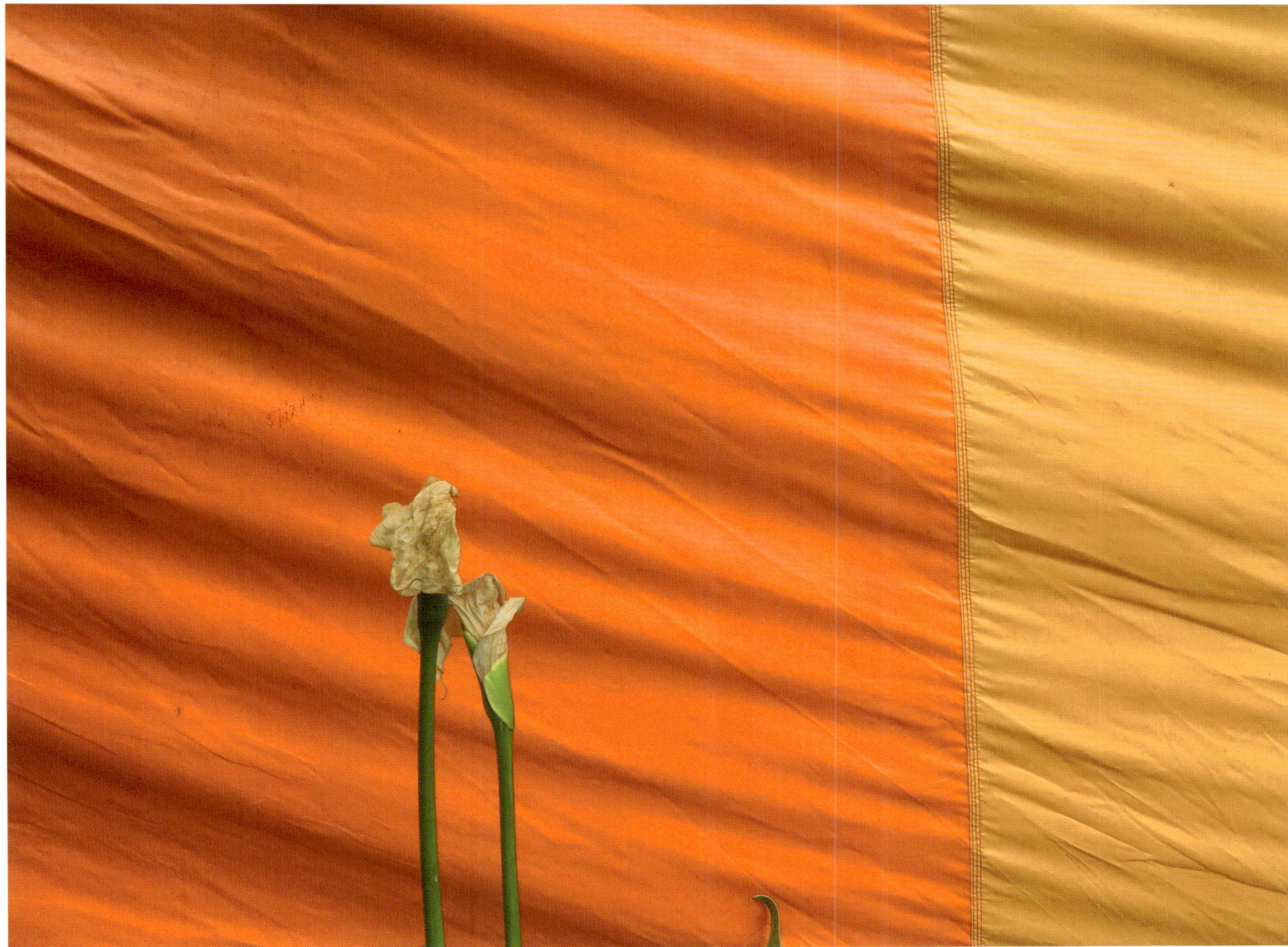

Georgina Ave.

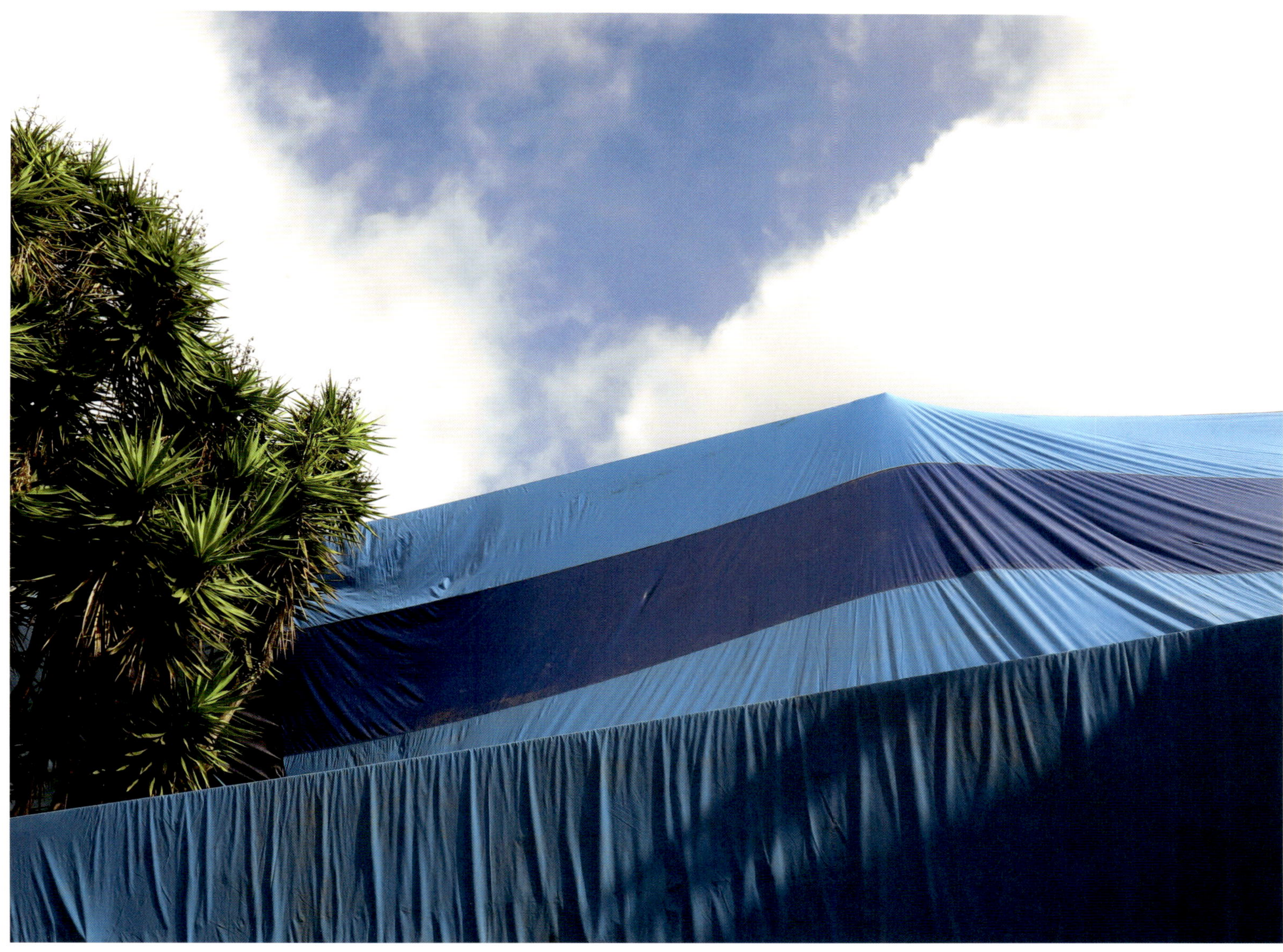

Riviera Ave.

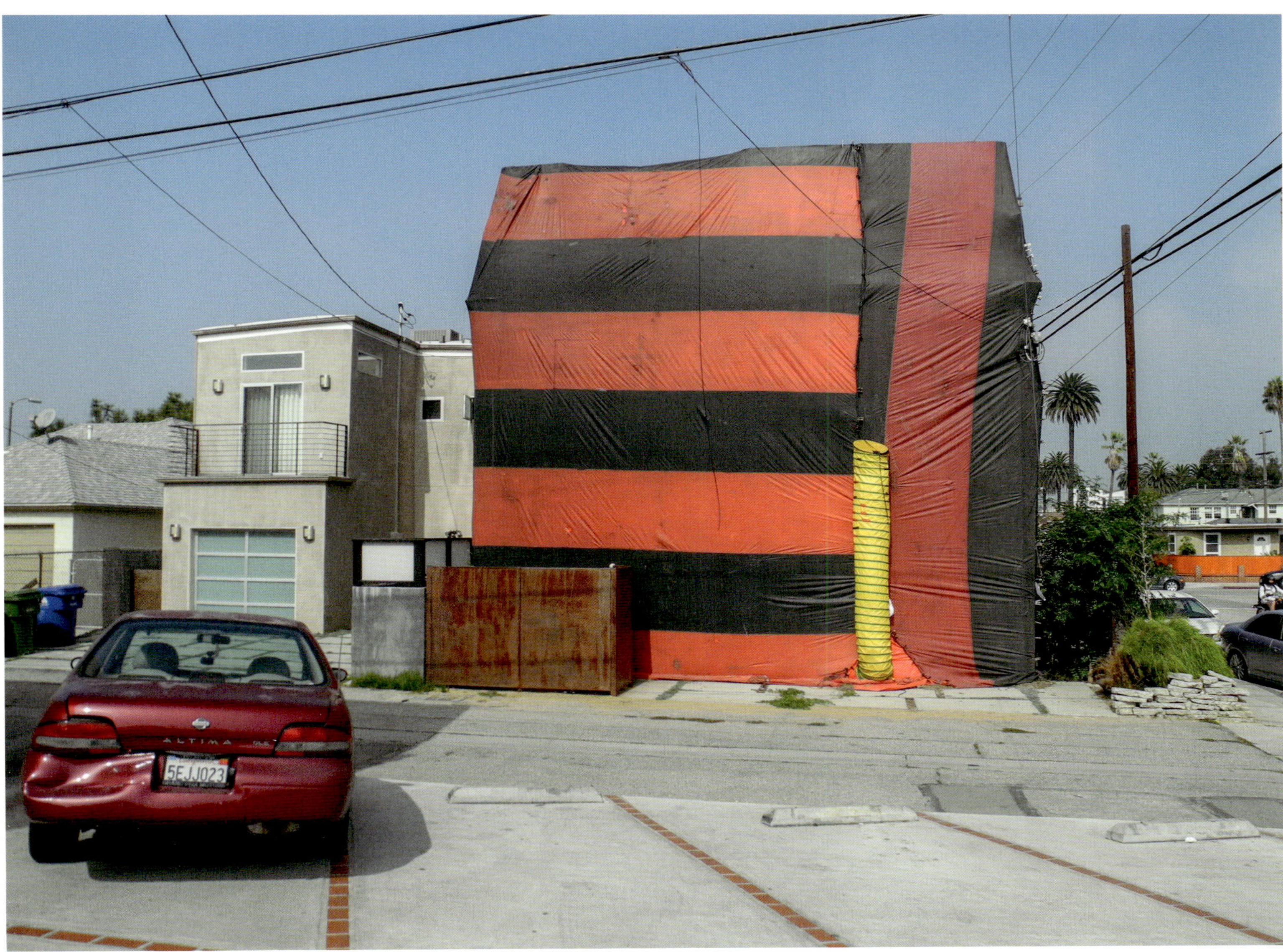

ALTIMA
5EJJ023

Westchester Prkwy.

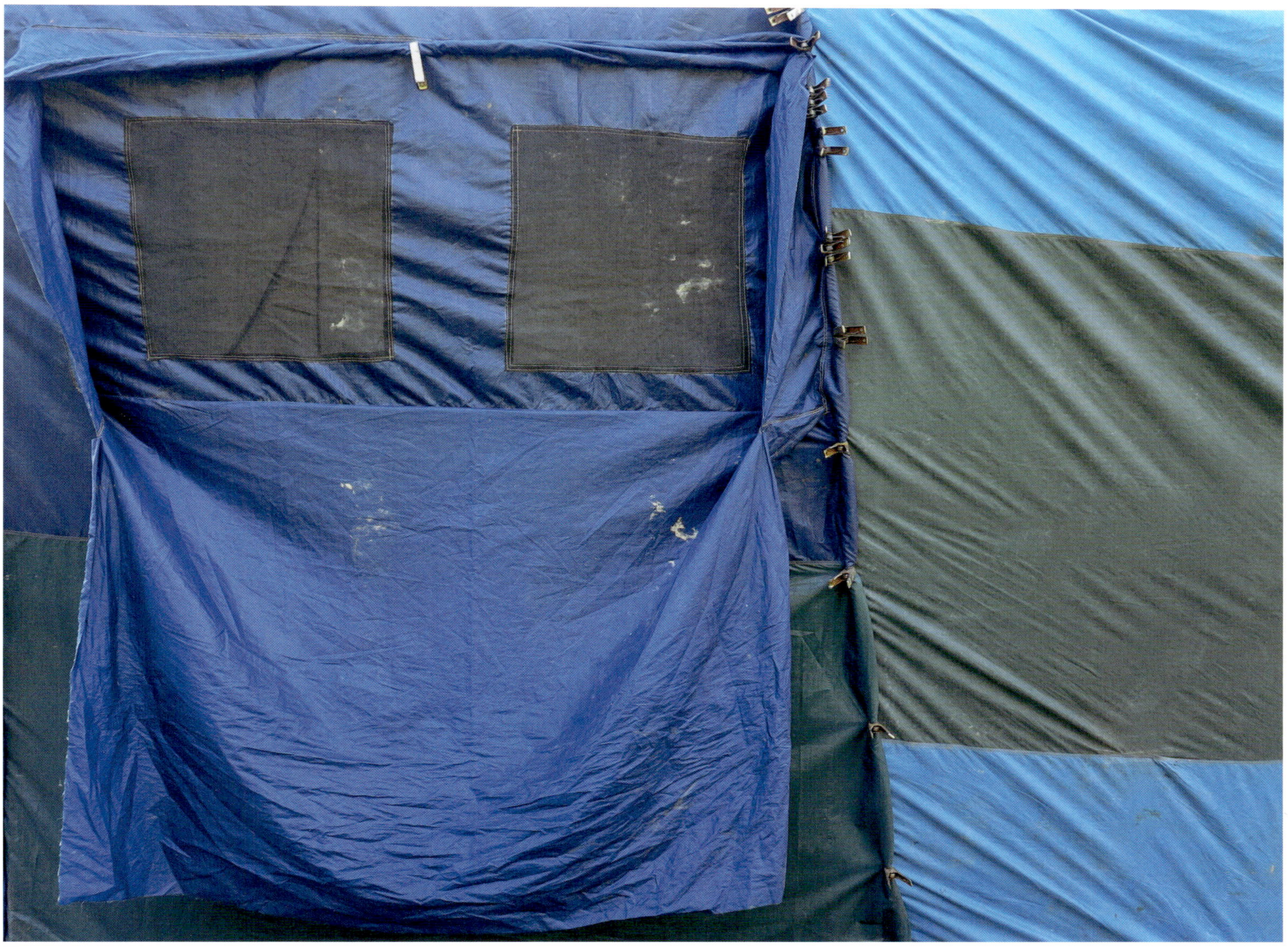

Washington Pl.

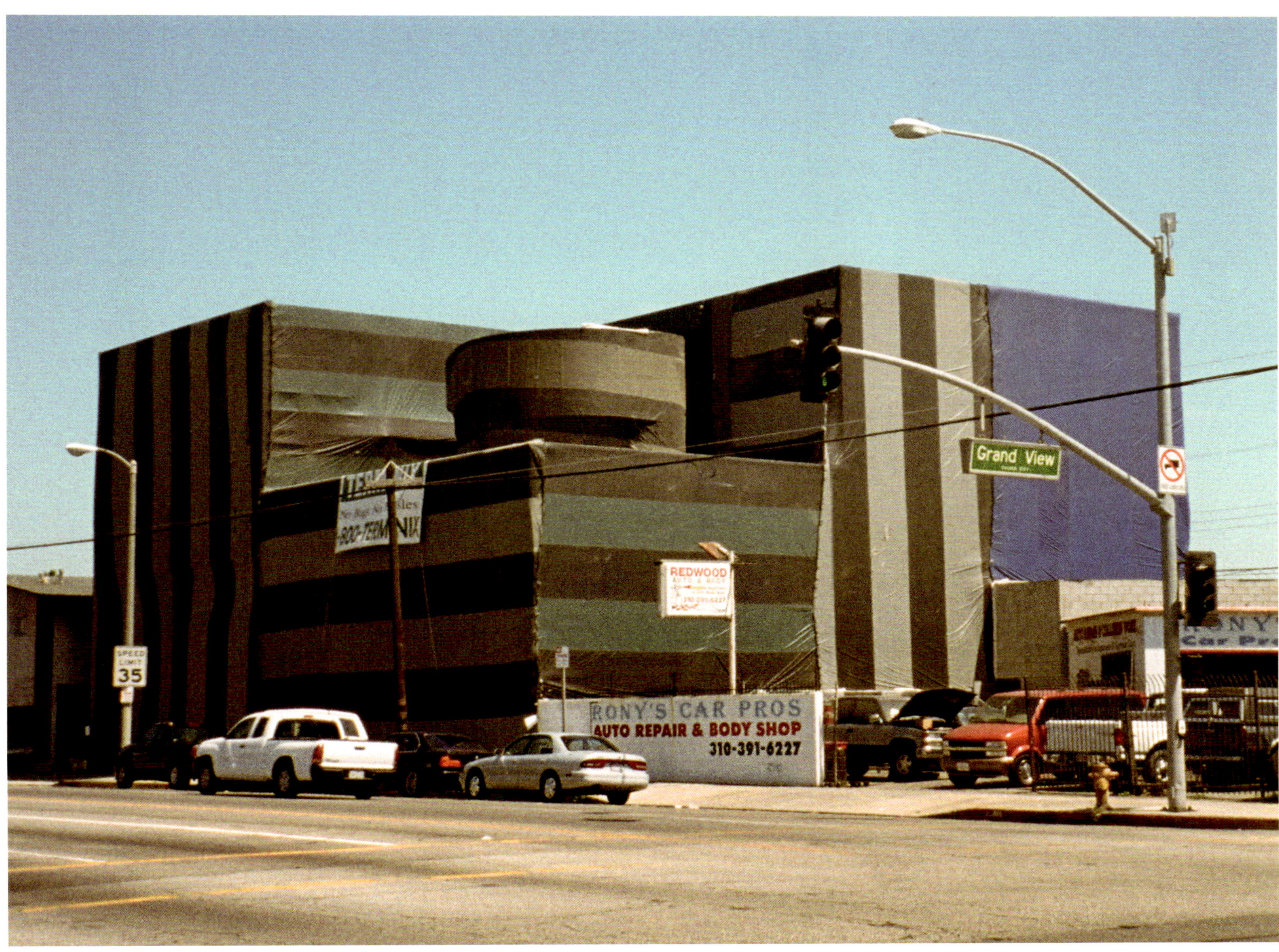
Grand View
SPEED LIMIT 35
REDWOOD
RONY'S CAR PROS
AUTO REPAIR & BODY SHOP
310-391-6227

Venice Blvd.

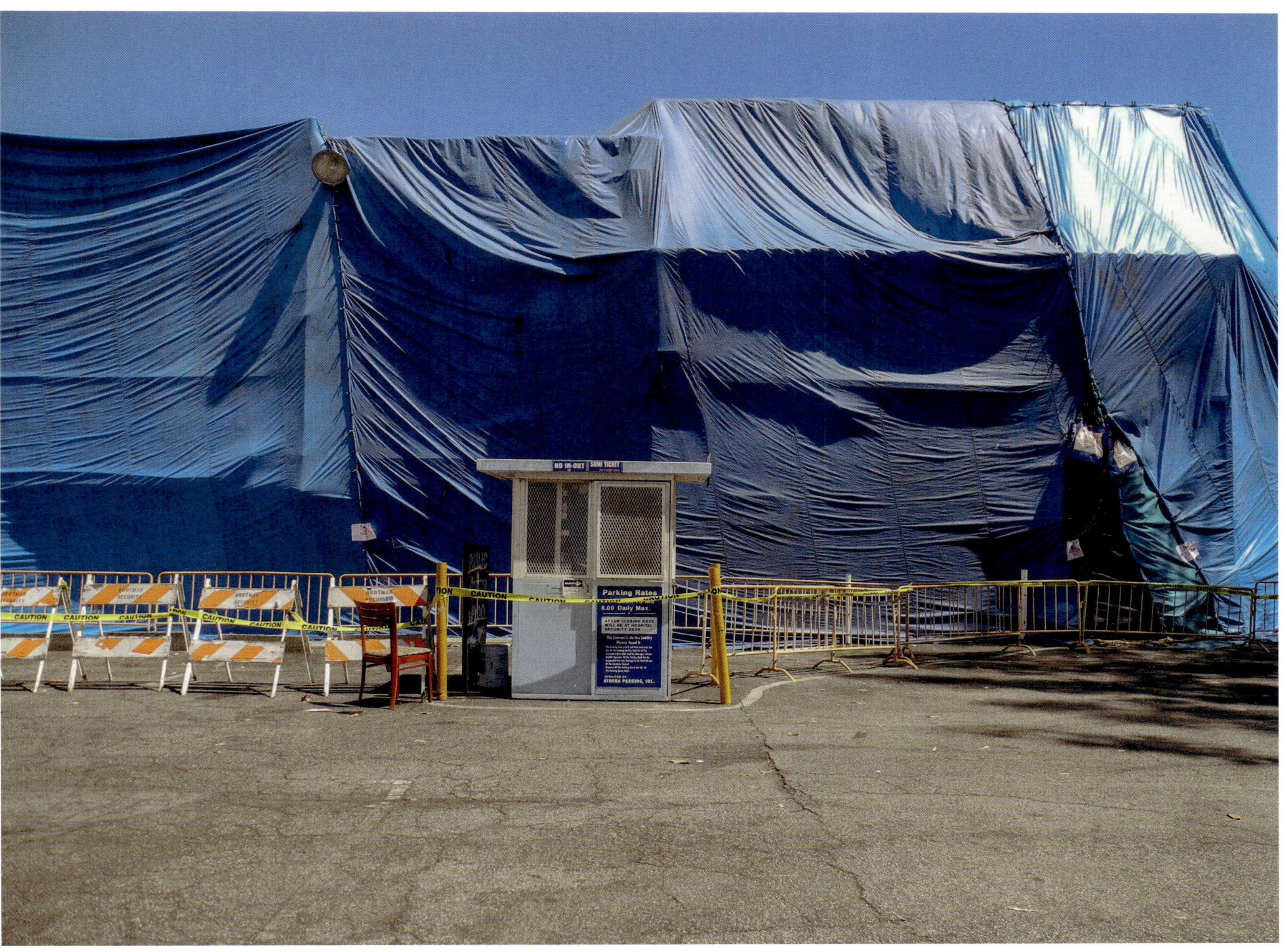
NO IN-OUT
SAME TICKET
CAUTION
Parking Rates
8.00 Daily Max.
AFTER CLOSING KEYS WILL BE AT HOSPITAL SECURITY DESK.
This Contract Limits Our Liability
Please Read It
OPERATED BY:
ATHENA PARKING, INC.

Pacific Coast Highway

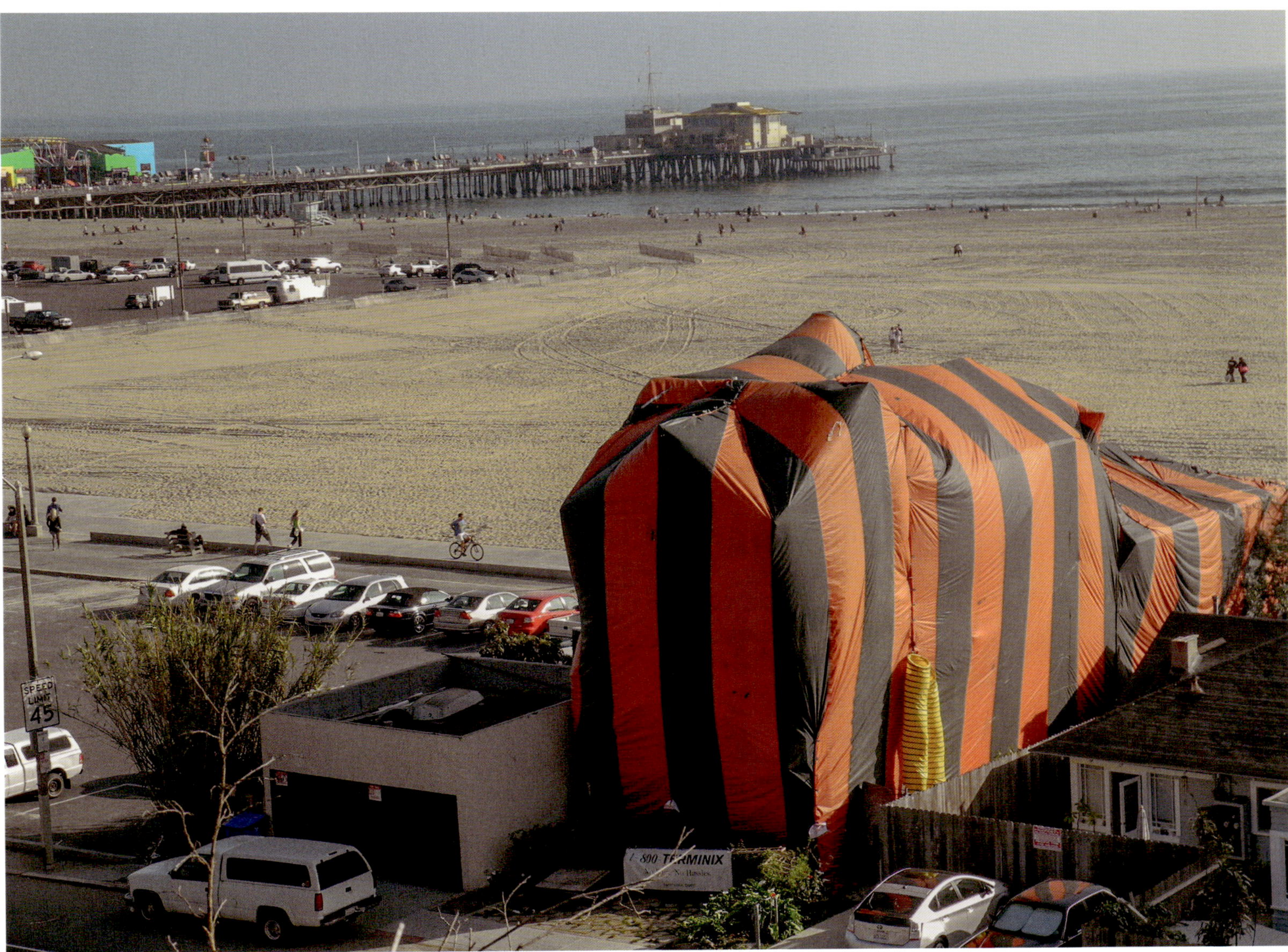
SPEED LIMIT
45
800-TERMINIX

Carlyle Ave.

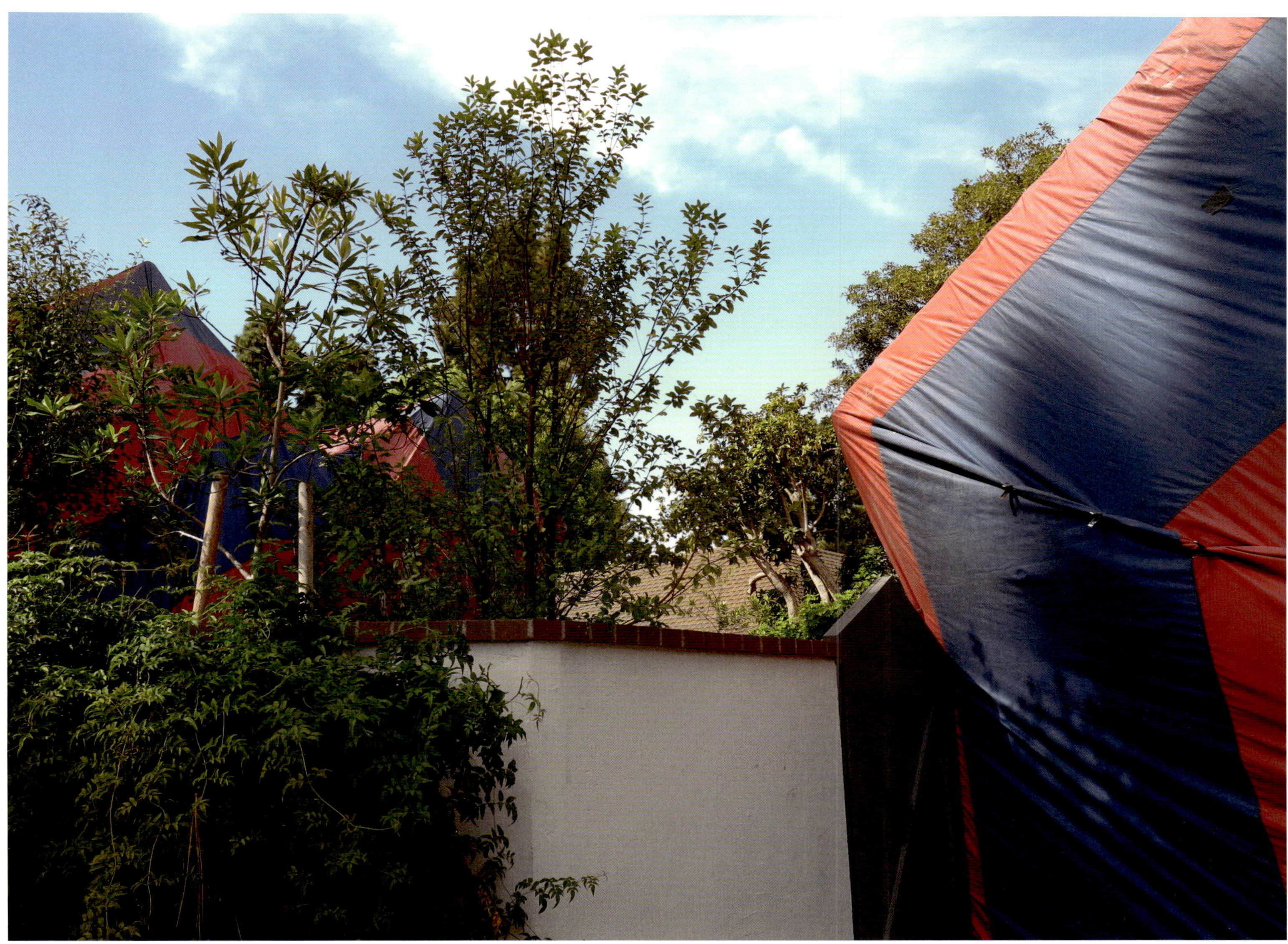

Bienveneda Ave.

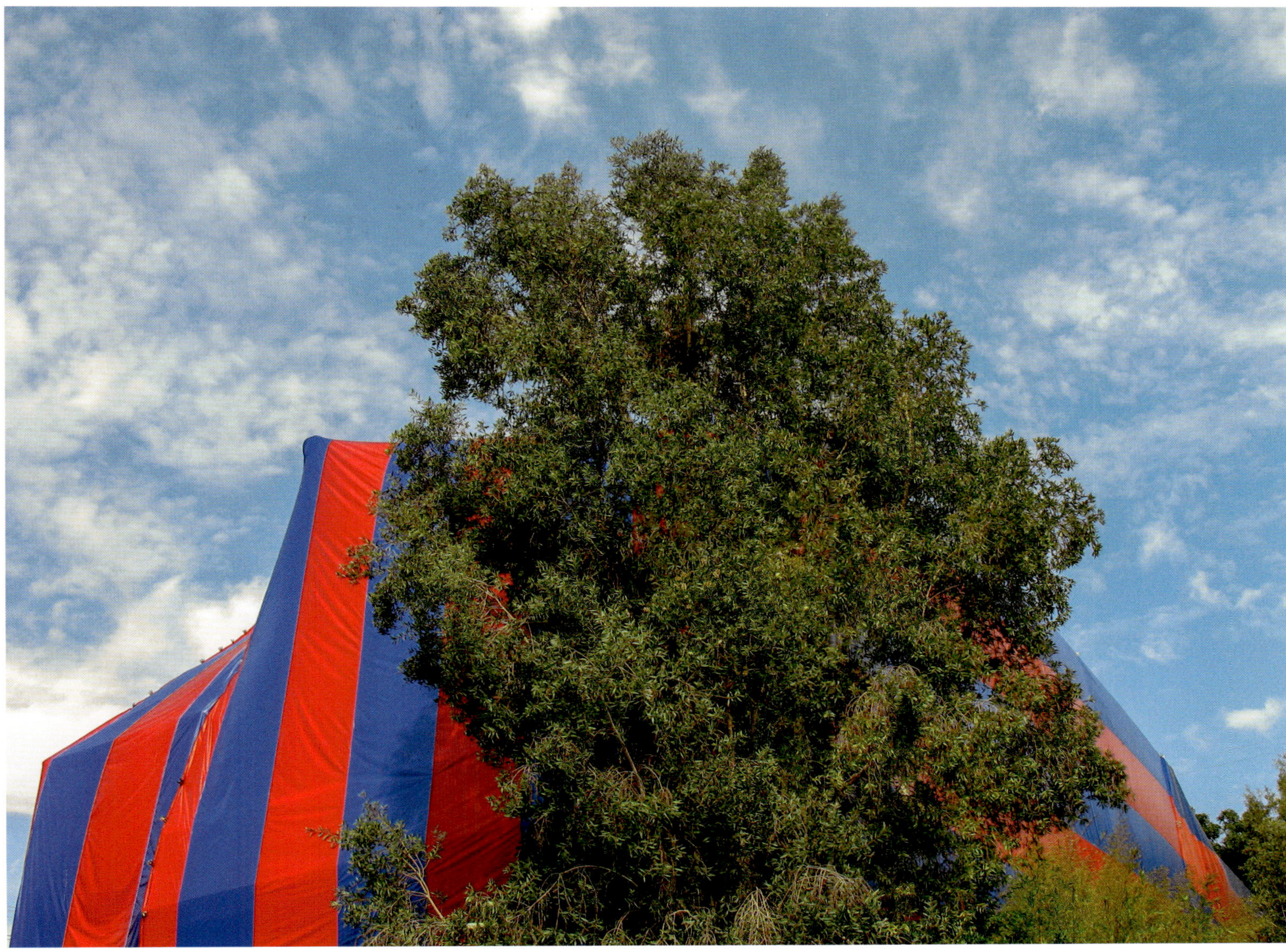

Brinkley Ave.

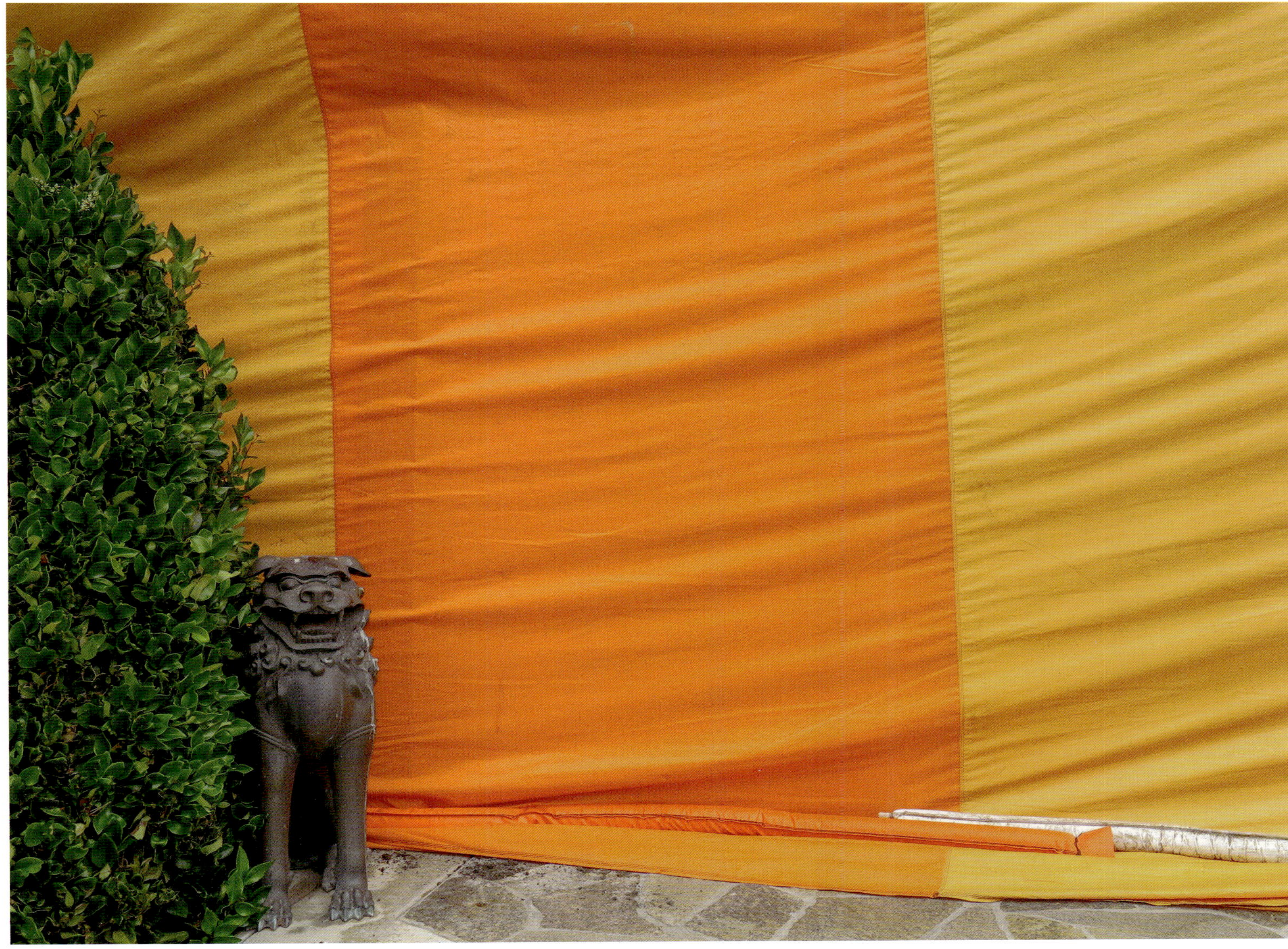

7th St.

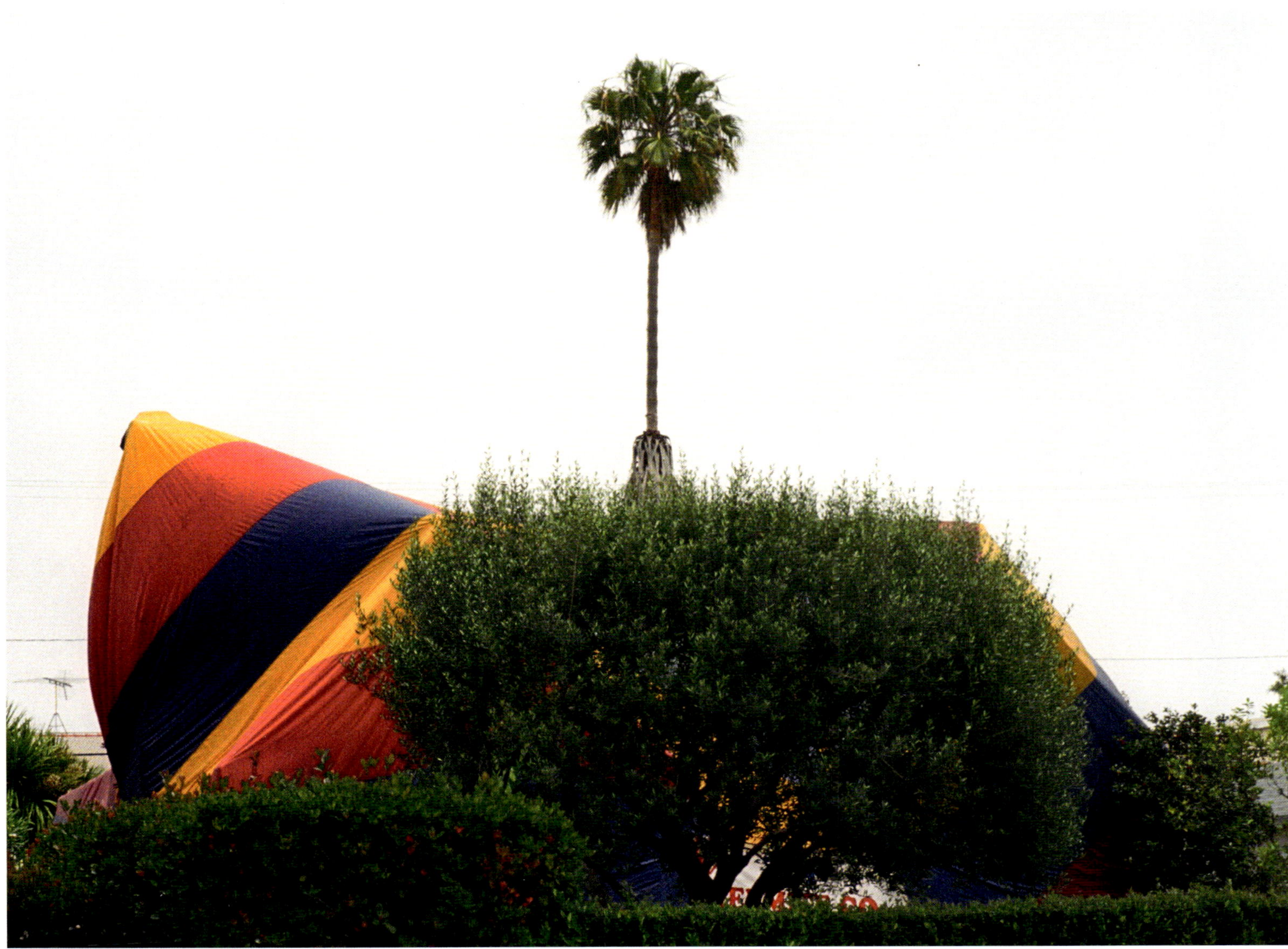

Venice Blvd.

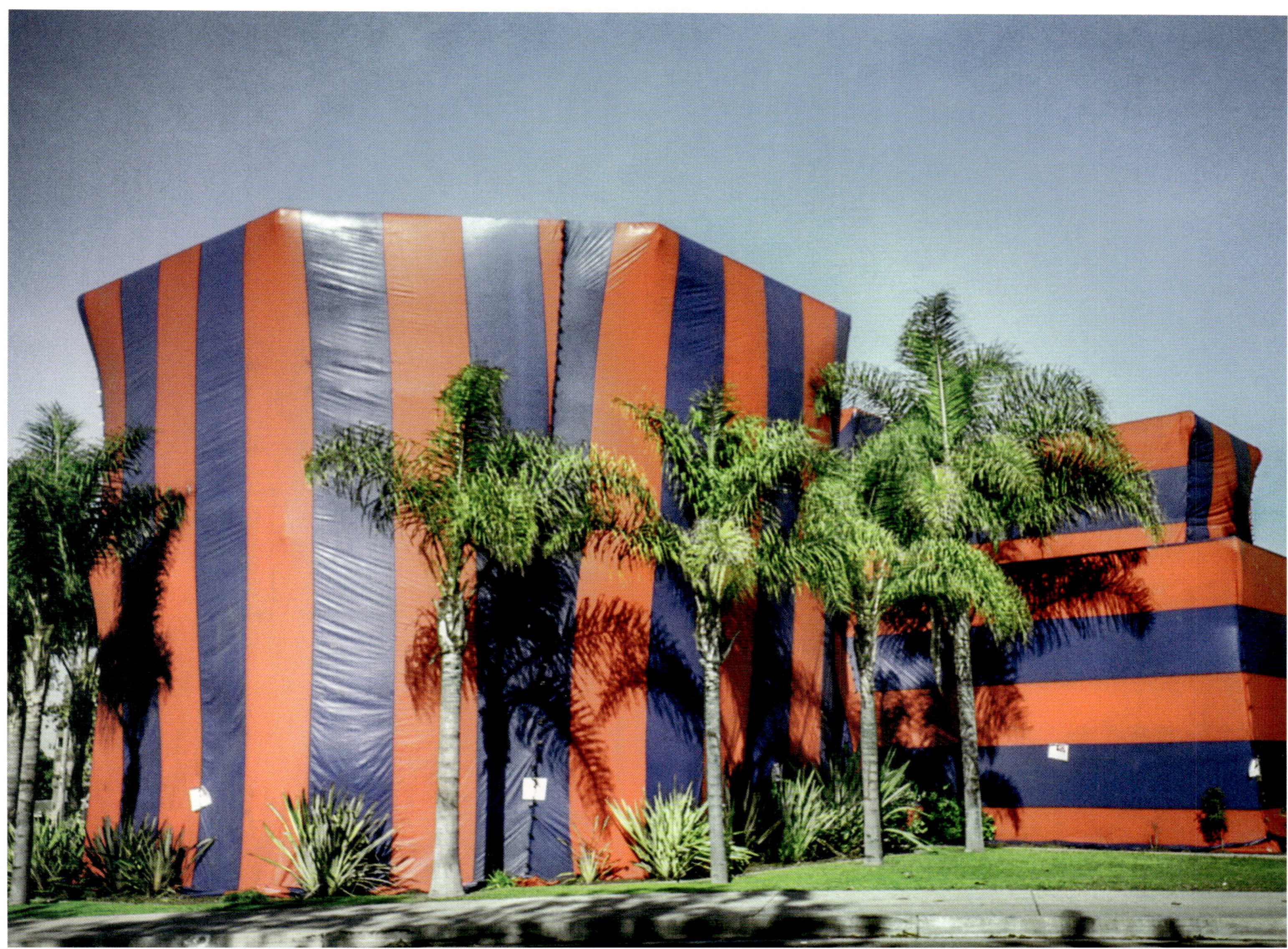

Greenfield Ave.

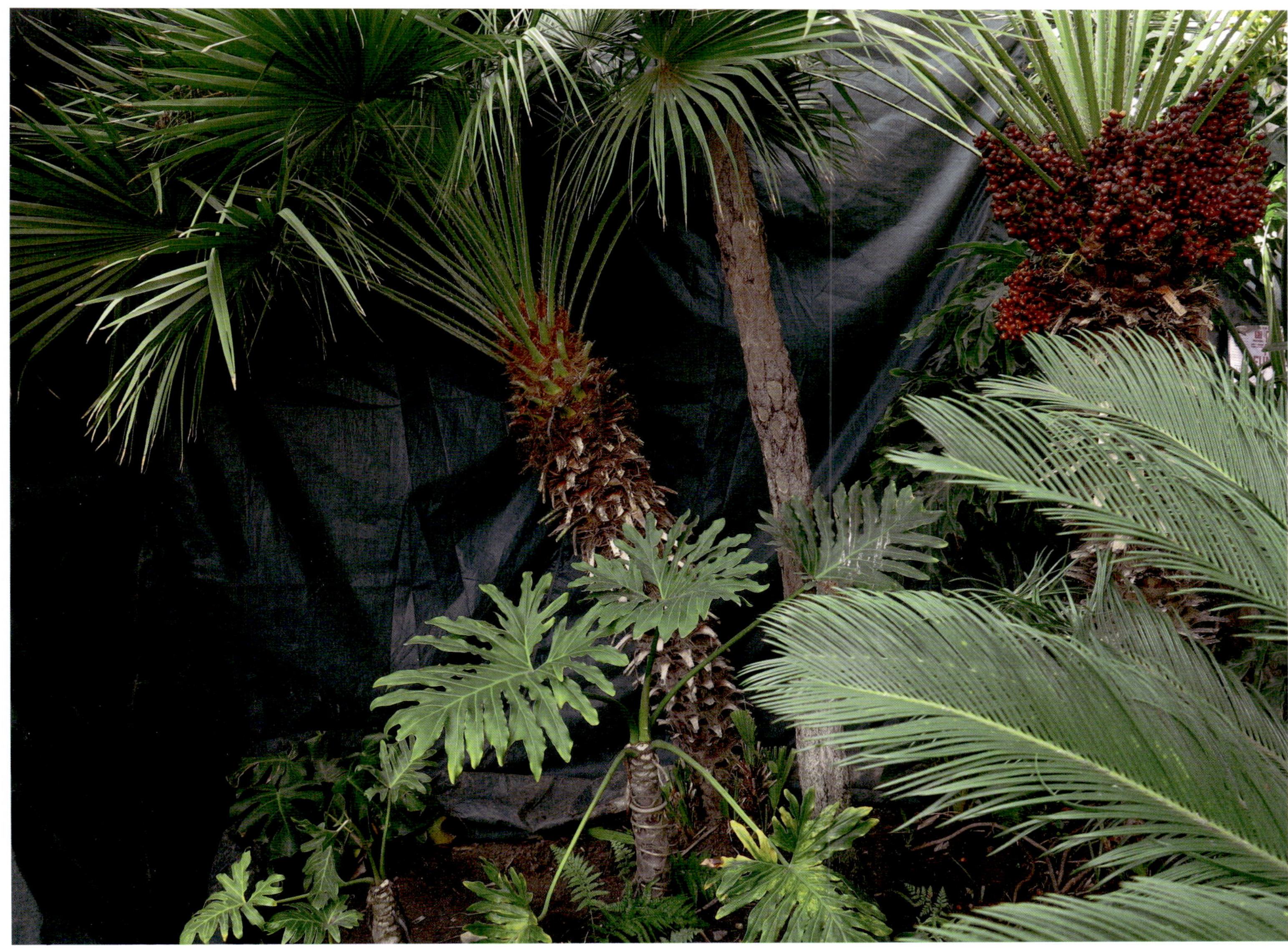

Allenford Ave.

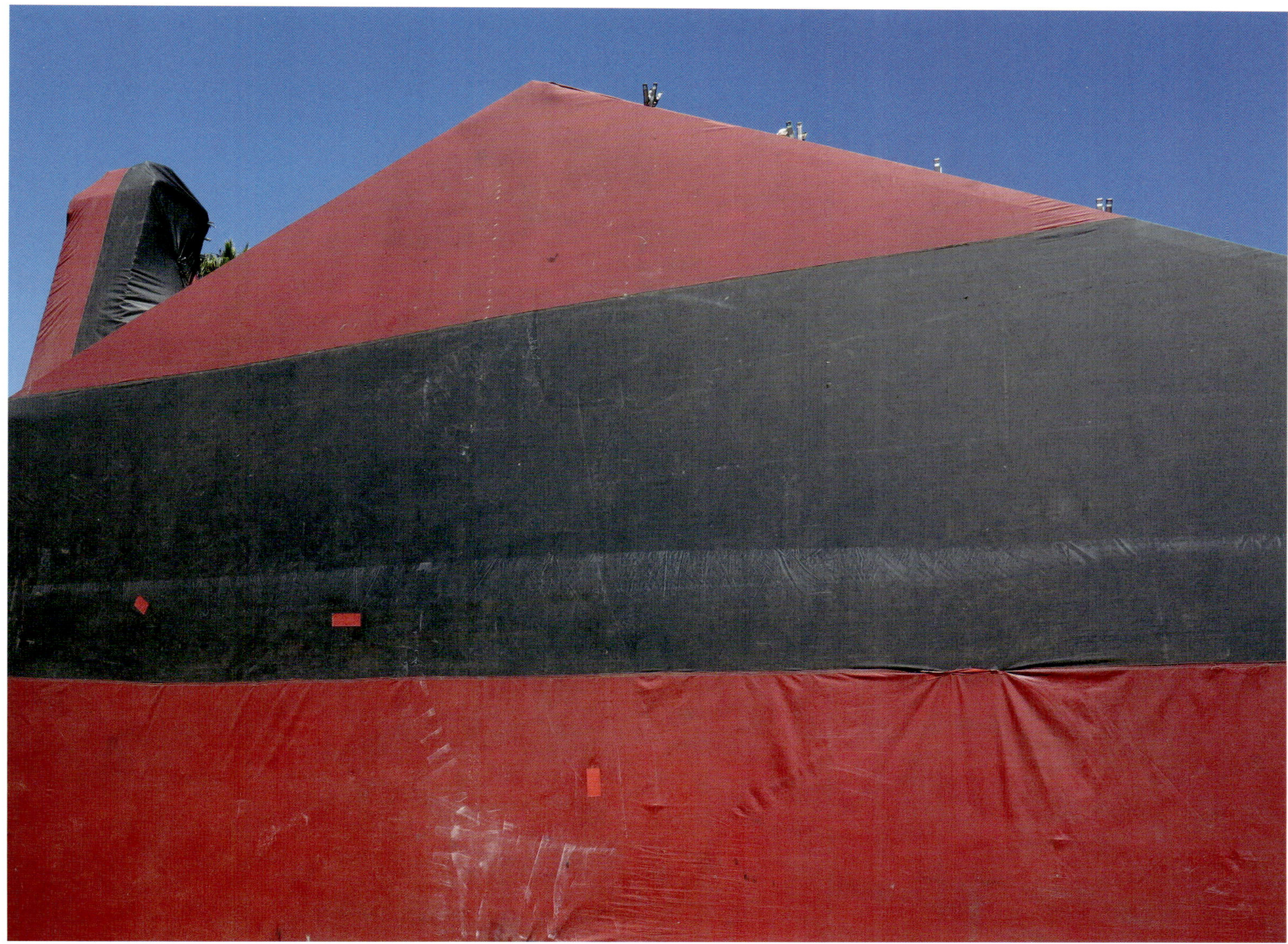

Capri Dr.

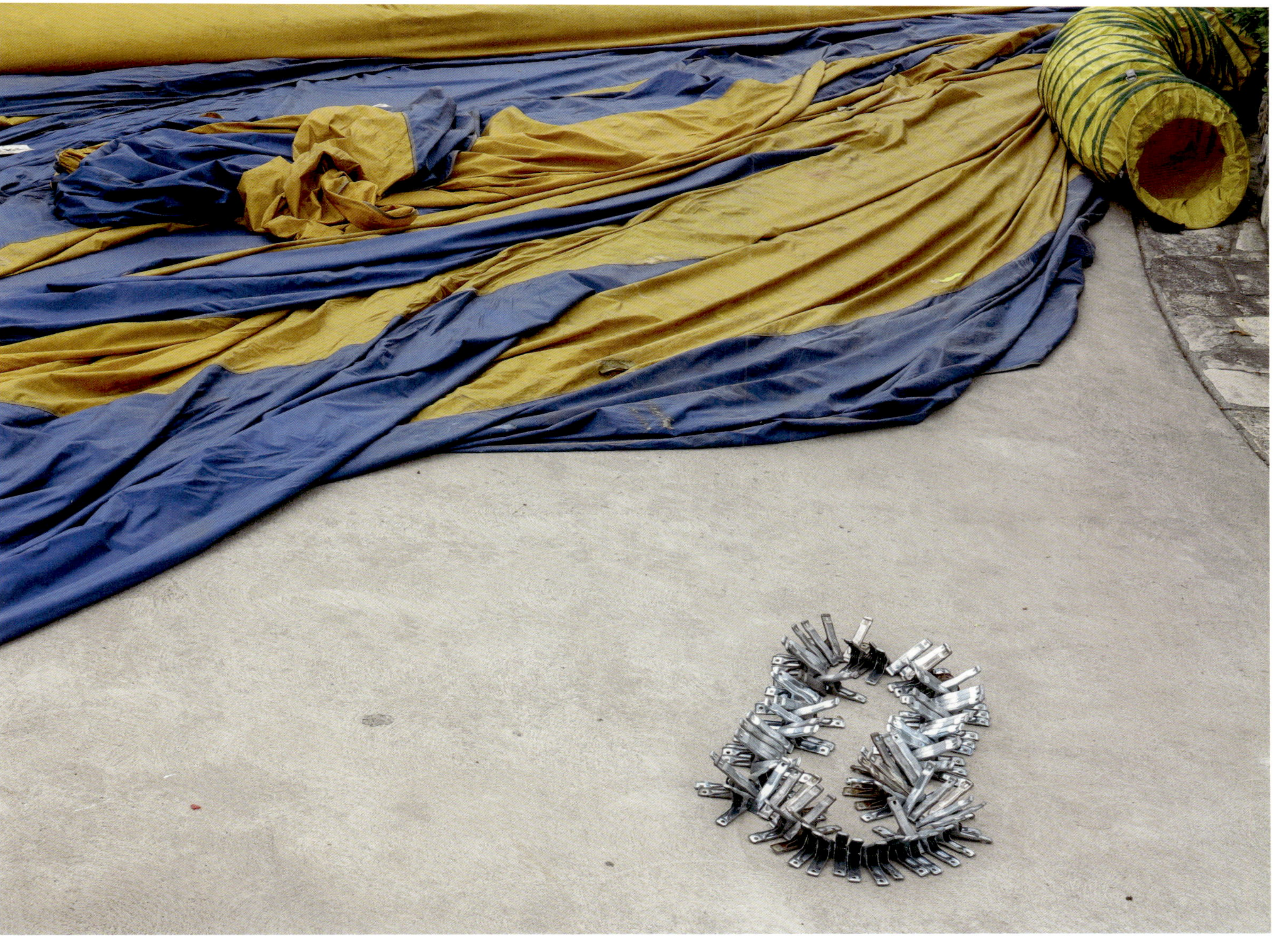

For Sam, Noah, Maya and Jeremy

Many thanks to:
D.J. Waldie, Clint Woodside, Lee Kaplan, Whitney Kaplan, Andrea Albertini, Jane Brown, Tricia Gabriel, Ken Brecher, Elsa Longhauser, Michael Shields, Miranda July, Louise Steinman, Helen Bartlett, Tony Bill, Bettina Hubby, Judith Guillemot, Jamie Rosenthal, Kate Greenberg, Pedro Riz a Porta, and Harlan Steinberger

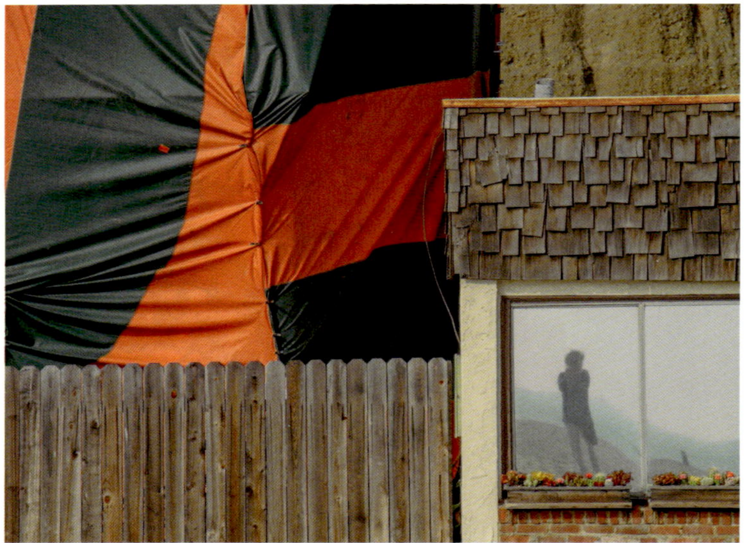

Randi Malkin Steinberger
No Circus

Edited by:
Randi Malkin Steinberger & Clint Woodside

Design by:
Clint Woodside

DAMIANI

Bologna, Italy
info@damianieditore.com
www.damianieditore.com

Printed in Faenza 2016 by Grafiche Damiani – Faenza Group, Italy.

ISBN 978-88-6208-480-2

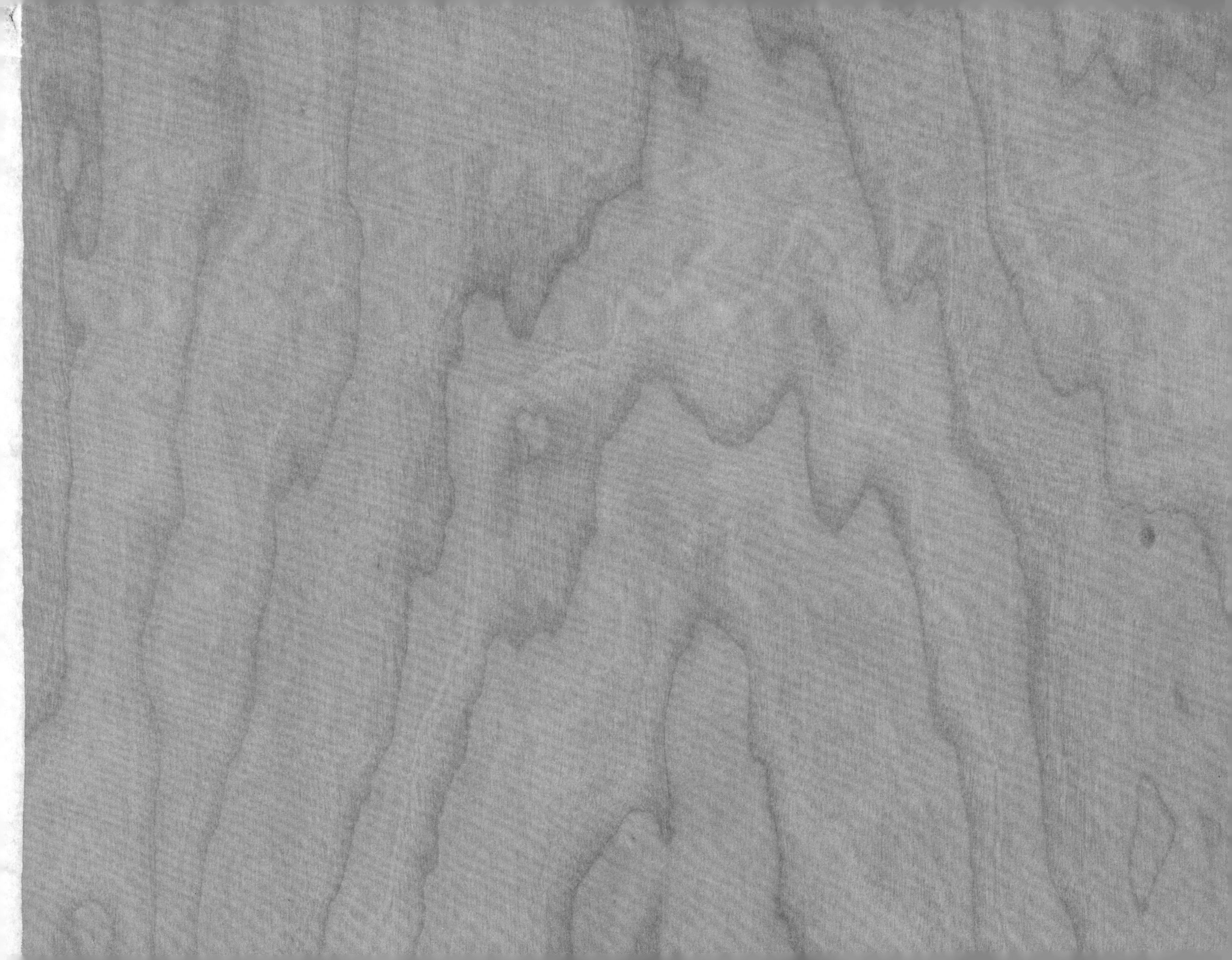

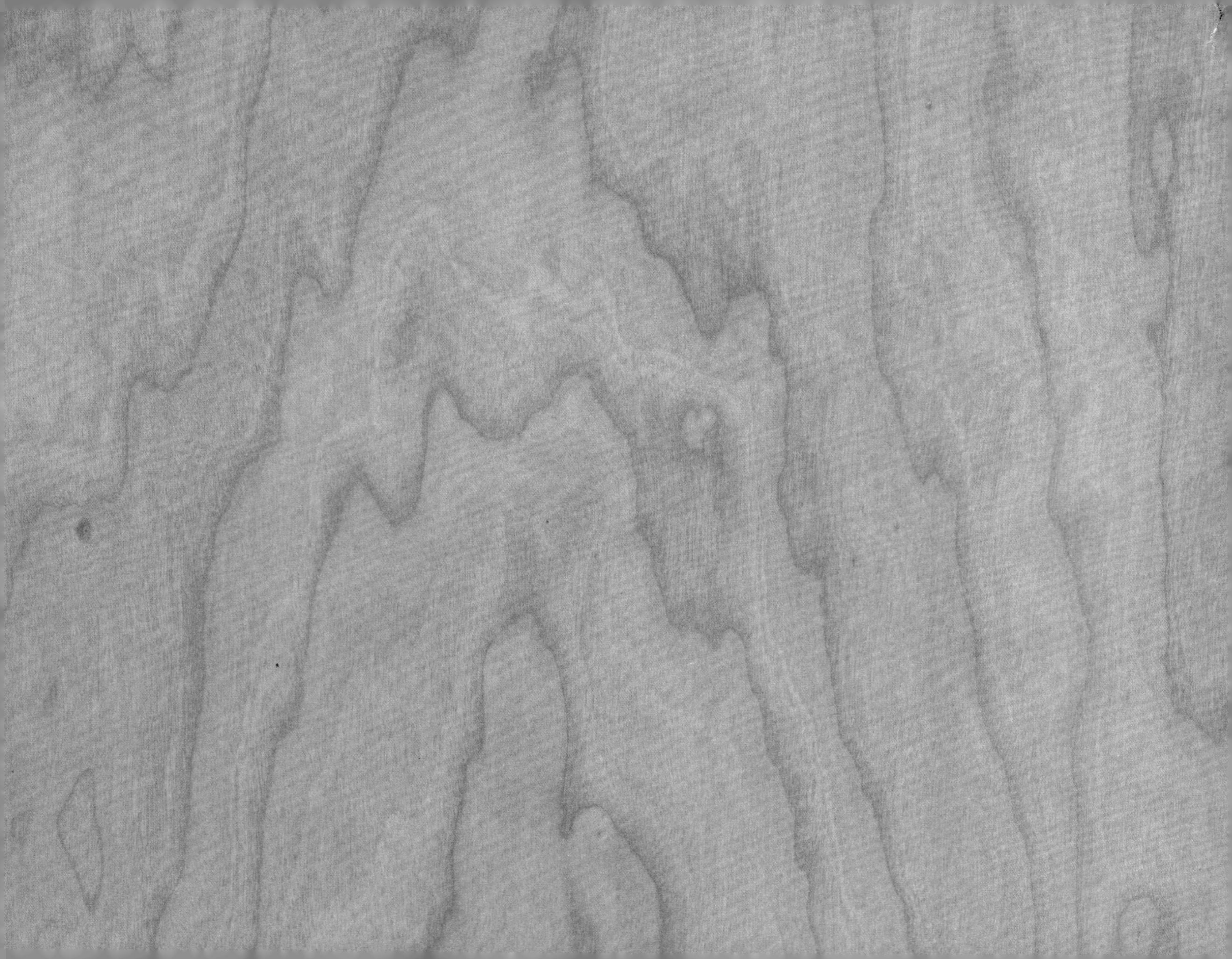